TRIO

LISTENING AND SPEAKING 1

The Intersection of Vocabulary, Listening, & Speaking

Alice Savage & Colin Ward

OXFORD
UNIVERSITY PRESS

OXFORD
UNIVERSITY PRESS

198 Madison Avenue
New York, NY 10016 USA

Great Clarendon Street, Oxford, OX2 6DP, United Kingdom

Oxford University Press is a department of the University of Oxford.
It furthers the University's objective of excellence in research, scholarship,
and education by publishing worldwide. Oxford is a registered trade
mark of Oxford University Press in the UK and in certain other countries

ISBN: 978 0 19 420306 7 STUDENT BOOK 1 WITH ONLINE PRACTICE PACK
ISBN: 978 0 19 420303 6 STUDENT BOOK 1 AS PACK COMPONENT
ISBN: 978 0 19 420321 0 ONLINE PRACTICE WEBSITE

Printed in China

This book is printed on paper from certified and well-managed sources

ACKNOWLEDGEMENTS

Cover Design: Yin Ling Wong

Illustrations by: Ben Hasler, p.3; Joe Taylor, pp.16, 76.

*The publishers would like to thank the following for their kind permission to reproduce
photographs*: p.1 specnaz/Shutterstock, OUP/Shutterstock/Eugenio Marongiu,
Caia Images/Superstock; p.4 Leren Lu/Getty Images, EyeEm/Alamy Stock
Photo, Olena Yakobchuk/Shutterstock, Cultura RM Exclusive/Nils Hendrik
Mueller/Getty Images, Foto Resources/Oriental Touch/AGE Fotostock, Monkey
Business Images/Shutterstock, mikkelwilliam/Getty Images, Dragon Images/
Shutterstock, arek_malang/Shutterstock; p.5 Asier Romero/Shutterstock,
OUP/Photodisc, David Wingate/Shutterstock, Anna/Alamy Stock Photo,
TungCheung/Shutterstock, OUP/Image Source, xPACIFICA/Alamy Stock
Photo, OUP/Shutterstock/Dariush M, OUP/Shutterstock/Sebastian Duda,
OUP/Shutterstock/Sergey Peterman, OUP/Shutterstock/gualtiero boffi,
specnaz/Shutterstock, jaboo2foto/Shutterstock, Fredrick Kippe/Alamy
Stock Photo, littleny/Shutterstock; p.6 Tetra Images/Superstock, Yellow Dog
Productions/Getty Images, KidStock/Getty Images, Adrian Sherratt/Alamy
Stock Photo, Neil McAllister/Alamy Stock Photo, Blend Images/Alamy Stock
Photo, Georgejmclittle/Shutterstock, Picture Partners/Alamy Stock Photo;
p.7 SGM/Shutterstock, OUP/Shutterstock/veronicagomezpola, Jim Havey/
Alamy Stock Photo, 1000 Words/Shutterstock, Blend Images/Superstock,
PhotoAlto/Alamy Stock Photo, Sam Diephuis/Getty Images, Roshan_NG/
Shutterstock, Dmitriy Shironosov/Alamy Stock Photo; p.8 Nils Jorgensen/
REX/Newscom, Monkey Business Images/Shutterstock, Neustockimages/
Getty Images, Jon Philpott Photography, capturing moments, people, life/
Getty Images, Milan Stojanovic/Shutterstock, OUP/Shutterstock/John A.
Anderson, Ro-Ma Stock Photography, Pixtal/Superstock, RIEGER Bertrand/
Hemis.fr/Superstock, KidStock/Getty Images; p.14 Asia Images Group/
Getty Images, Ulli Seer/LOOK-foto/Getty Images, Hero Images/Getty Images,
Image Source/Superstock; p.16 antoniodiaz/Shutterstock, wavebreakmedia/
Shutterstock, Jacob Lund/Shutterstock, bikeriderlondon/Shutterstock; p.19
skynesher/Getty Images, Christian Bertrand/Shutterstock, Wavebreak Media
ltd/Alamy Stock Photo; p.20 skynesher/Getty Images, Shotshop GmbH/
Alamy Stock Photo, SpeedKingz/Shutterstock, Image Source/Getty Images,
Hero Images Inc./Alamy Stock Photo, PhotoAlto/Superstock, Blend Images
- Dave and Les Jacobs/Getty Images, Daniel Pangbourne/Getty Images; p.22
David Schaffer/Getty Images, Alexander Raths/Shutterstock, Philip Game/
Alamy Stock Photo, Christopher Robbins/Getty Images, Jessica Peterson/
Getty Images, Antonio Guillem/Shutterstock, MBI/Alamy Stock Photo;
p.24 SOMOS/Superstock, Lisa F. Young/Alamy Stock Photo; p.32 StockLite/
Shutterstock, STICHELBAUT Benoit/Hemis.fr/Superstock, Pietro Scozzari/
age fotostock/Superstock, Brett Carlsen/Getty Images, Britain on View/Getty
Images, Thomas Barwick/Getty Images, JTB Media Creation, Inc./Alamy Stock
Photo, Christian Bertrand/Shutterstock; p.34 oreanto/Shutterstock, Frans
Lemmens/Getty Images, MBI/Alamy Stock Photo, Ian Allenden/Alamy Stock
Photo, Design Pics Inc/Alamy Stock Photo, Cultura Limited/Superstock,
Ian Dagnall/Alamy Stock Photo, Paul Burns/Getty Images; p.44 B.O'Kane/
Alamy Stock Photo, Alexey Arkhipov/Shutterstock, Wavebreak Media ltd/
Alamy Stock Photo, Matt Mawson/Getty Images, JGI/Jamie Grill/Getty Images,
Peathegee Inc/Getty Images, Caiaimage/Sam Edwards/Getty Images, Ian G
Dagnall/Alamy Stock Photo; p.46 Wladimir Bulgar/Science Photo Library,
VCG/VCG via Getty Images, China Images/Alamy Stock Photo, SolStock/Getty
Images, David J. Green/Alamy Stock Photo, studiocasper/Getty Images, Ian
G Dagnall/Alamy Stock Photo, Satyrenko/Shutterstock; p.49 Radiokafka/
Shutterstock, Detlev Van Ravenswaay/Science Photo Library, AF archive/
Alamy Stock Photo; p.57 Fuse/Getty Images, apiguide/Shutterstock, Hongqi
Zhang/Alamy Stock Photo; p.58 Darren Hubley/Shutterstock, Africa Studio/
Shutterstock, Anatoliy Cherkas/Shutterstock, kampolz/Shutterstock, Perart/
Shutterstock, Elena de las Heras/Getty Images, James O'Sullivan/Alamy Stock
Photo; p.59 José Fuste Raga/AGE fotostock, TommL/Getty Images, Kipling
Brock/Shutterstock, Lissandra Melo/Shutterstock; p.60 JGI/Jamie Grill/Getty
Images, Teresa De Paul/Getty Images, kekartash/Shutterstock, BirchTree/
Alamy Stock Photo, ambrozinio/Shutterstock, StockStudio/Shutterstock,
Design Pics Inc/Alamy Stock Photo, Image Source/Alamy Stock Photo; p.63
Jon Bilous/Shutterstock, Luciano Mortula/Shutterstock; p.70 Jouan Rius/
Nautrepl.com, Peter ten Broecke/Getty Images, Pietro Scozzari/age fotostock/
Superstock, Slawomir Kruz/Shutterstock, Olga Danylenko/Shutterstock,
Mike Dobel/Masterfile, LOOK Die Bildagentur der Fotografen GmbH/Alamy
Stock Photo, Gallo Images/Superstock; p.72 DESCAMPS Simon/hemi/AGE
Fotostock, loridambrosio/Getty Images, bikeriderlondon/Shutterstock,
photka/Shutterstock, Mitch Diamond/Alamy Stock Photo, Alexander Raths/
Shutterstock, Pressmaster/Shutterstock, Syda Productions/Shutterstock; p.82
Hongqi Zhang/Alamy Stock Photo, The Irish Image Collection/Superstock,
migstock/Alamy Stock Photo, Image Source/Superstock, Lev Dolgachov/
Alamy Stock Photo, Hero Images/Getty Images, JGI/Tom Grill/Getty Images,
Mitchell Funk/Getty Images; p.84 Brittarose/Shutterstock, Jim West/Alamy
Stock Photo, Asia Images Group Pte Ltd/Alamy Stock Photo, vectorfusionart/
Shutterstock, OUP/Neus Grandia, OUP/Shutterstock/Simone van den Berg,
Vitalii Nesterchuk/Shutterstock, MONTICO Lionel/Hemis.fr/Superstock; p.95
bokan/Shutterstock, BJI/Blue Jean Images/Getty Images, Moxie Productions/
Getty Images; p.96 altrendo images/Getty Images, TongRo Images/Alamy
Stock Photo, Blend Images/Superstock, BURGER/PHANIE/AGE fotostock, Tony
Tallec/Alamy Stock Photo, Iakov Filimonov/Shutterstock, Fuse/Getty Images;
p.98 OUP/Blend Images, Jeka/Shutterstock, Robert Kneschke/Shutterstock,
Grigory Lugovoy/Shutterstock, Becky Stares/Shutterstock, Peter Dazeley/
Getty Images, Gary John Norman/Getty Images, Glow Wellness/Superstock;
p.102 Blend Images/Alamy Stock Photo, Friedrich Stark/Alamy Stock Photo;
p.108 Simon Battensby/Getty Images, Demjanovich Vadim/Shutterstock,
shooter/Alamy Stock Photo, jejim/Shutterstock, Zoonar t schneider/AGE
fotostock, trek6500/Shutterstock, Christopher Meder/Shutterstock, Ann
Haritonenko/Shutterstock; p.110 Lumi Images/Robert Niedring/Getty Images,
Fuse/Getty Images, stockernumber2/Shutterstock, Lichtmeister/Shutterstock,
Rawpixel.com/Shutterstock, Kenishirotie/Shutterstock, PhotosLifestyle/
Shutterstock, Joseph Branston/Digital Camera Magazine via Getty Images;
p.120 Blend Images/Alamy Stock Photo, GraficallyMinded/Alamy Stock Photo,
Photosindia.com/Superstock, TonyV3112/Shutterstock, OUP/Image Source,
Iakov Filimonov/Shutterstock, antoniodiaz/Shutterstock, Claude Dagenais/
Getty Images; p.122 red mango/Shutterstock, Bella Falk/Alamy Stock Photo,
Barry Austin Photography/Getty Images, Kevin Britland/Alamy Stock Photo,
Kumar Sriskandan/Alamy Stock Photo, Fancy Collection/Superstock, Monkey
Business Images/Shutterstock, Andrey_Popov/Shutterstock; pp.31, 43, 55, 69,
81, 93, 107, 119, 131 Hero Images/Getty Images.

REVIEWERS

We would like to acknowledge the following individuals for their input during the development of the series:

Aubrey Adrianson
Ferris State University
U.S.A.

Sedat Akayoğlu
Middle East Technical University
Turkey

Mahmoud Al-Salah
University of Dammam
Saudi Arabia

Lisa Alton
University of Alberta
Canada

Robert J. Ashcroft
Tokai University
Japan

Ibrahim Atay
Izzet Baysal University
Turkey

Türkan Aydin
Çanakkale Onsekiz Mart University
Turkey

Pelin Tekinalp Cakmak
Marmara University, School of Foreign Languages
Turkey

Raul Cantu
Austin Community College
United States

Karen E. Caldwell
Higher Colleges of Technology, Women's College, U.A.E.

Danielle Chircop
Kaplan International English
U.S.A.

Jennifer Chung
Gwangju ECC
South Korea

Elaine Cockerham
Higher College of Technology
Oman

Abdullah Coskun
Abant Izzet Baysal University
Turkey

Stephanie da Costa Mello
Glendale Community College
U.S.A.

Travis Cote
Tamagawa University
Japan

Linda Crocker
University of Kentucky
U.S.A.

Ian Daniels
Smart ELT
Japan

Adem Onur Fedai
Fatih University Preparatory School
Turkey

Gail Fernandez
Bergen Community College
U.S.A.

Theresa Garcia de Quevedo
Geos Boston English Language School
U.S.A.

Greg Holloway
Kyushu Institute of Technology
Japan

Elizabeth Houtrow
Soongsil University
South Korea

Shu-Chen Huang
National Chengchi University
Taipei City

Patricia Ishill
Union County College
U.S.A.

Ji Hoon Kim
Independence English Institute
South Korea

Masakazu Kimura
Katoh Gakuen Gyoshu High School/Nihon University
Japan

Georgios-Vlasios Kormpas
Al Yamamah University/SILC
Saudi Arabia

Ece Selva Küçükoğlu
METU School of Foreign Languages
Turkey

Ji-seon Lee
Jeong English Campus
South Korea

Sang-lee Lee
Kangleong Community Language Center
South Korea

Zee Eun Lim
Reader's Mate
South Korea

James MacDonald
Aspire Language Academy
Kaohsiung City

Margaret Martin
Xavier University
U.S.A.

Murray McMahon
University of Alberta
Canada

Chaker Ali Mhamdi
Al Buraimi University College
Oman

Elizabeth R. Neblett
Union County College
U.S.A.

Eileen O'Brien
Khalifa University of Science, Technology and Research
U.A.E.

Fernanda Ortiz
Center for English as a Second Language at University of Arizona
U.S.A.

Ebru Osborne
Yildiz Technical University
Turkey

Joshua Pangborn
Kaplan International
U.S.A.

John Peloghitis
Tokai University
Japan

Erkan Kadir Şimşek
Akdeniz University Manavgat Vocational College
Turkey

Veronica Struck
Sussex County Community College
U.S.A.

Clair Taylor
Gifu Shotoku Gakuen University
Japan

Melody Traylor
Higher Colleges of Technology
U.A.E.

Whitney Tullos
Intrax
U.S.A.

Sabiha Tunc
Baskent University English Language Department
Turkey

John Vogels
Dubai Men's College
U.A.E.

Pingtang Yen
Eden Institute
Taichung City

Author Acknowledgments

We would like to thank the many people who were involved in the development of *Trio Listening & Speaking*. It would not have been successful without a wonderful team by our side. Sharon Sargent, Tracey Gibbons, Sandra Frith, Marc Goozée, Keyana Shaw, and Eliza Jensen, thanks to all of you for your involvement and dedication to this project.

Trio Listening & Speaking 1 was a wonderful journey to be on, and we learned so much in the process of bringing theory into practice. We are dedicated to our amazing students at Lone Star College–North Harris, who inspire us every day to continue to create the materials we do.

—A.S. and C.W.

CONTENTS

READINESS UNIT Vocabulary, Listening, & Speaking pages 1–18

UNIT 1 People pages 19–56

CHAPTER	▲ VOCABULARY	▲▲ LISTENING	▲▲▲ SPEAKING
1 **Are You Ready?** page 20	Oxford 2000 ✦ words to talk about school	Listening for questions and statements Listening for directions	Practicing stress on two-syllable adjectives Making small talk with new classmates
2 **Do You Like Music?** page 32	Oxford 2000 ✦ words to talk about interests	Listening to learn about activities people like Listening for a speaker's questions	Practicing stress on nouns Sharing interests with others
3 **Do You Want to Meet for Coffee?** page 44	Oxford 2000 ✦ words to talk about places on campus	Listening for *here* and *there* Listening for sequence words	Practicing linking with the schwa /ə/ sound Making plans to get together with classmates

UNIT WRAP UP Extend Your Skills page 56

UNIT 2 Places pages 57–94

CHAPTER	▲ VOCABULARY	▲▲ LISTENING	▲▲▲ SPEAKING
4 **What's Your New Place Like?** page 58	Oxford 2000 ✦ words to talk about living preferences	Listening for hesitations Listening for reasons	Practicing intonation of choice questions Surveying others about their living preferences
5 **What Can You Do There?** page 70	Oxford 2000 ✦ words to talk about outdoor activities	Listening for time Listening for place	Practicing reductions of *can* in *wh-* questions Describing a place tourists can visit

Welcome to Trio Listening and Speaking

Building Better Communicators . . . From the Beginning

Trio Listening and Speaking includes three levels of Student Books, Online Practice, and Teacher Support.

Level 1/CEFR A1

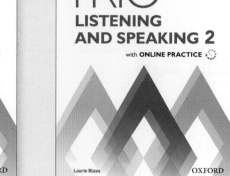

Level 2/CEFR A2

Level 3/CEFR B1

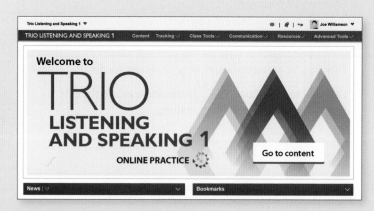

Essential Digital Content with Classroom Resources for Teachers

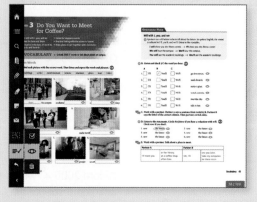

Classroom Presentation Tool

Trio Listening and Speaking's contextualized vocabulary instruction, academic listening strategies, and focus on pronunciation provide students with the tools they need for successful academic listening and speaking at the earliest stages of language acquisition.

Vocabulary Based On the Oxford 2000 🔑 Keywords

Trio Listening and Speaking's vocabulary is based on the 2,000 most important and useful words to learn at the early stages of language learning, making content approachable for low-level learners.

Practical Listening and Speaking Instruction

Conversation and academic listening sections prepare learners for real situations, while a focus on pronunciation helps students communicate successfully.

Readiness Unit

For added flexibility, each level of *Trio Listening and Speaking* begins with an optional Readiness Unit to provide fundamental English tools for beginning students.

INSIDE EACH CHAPTER

▲ VOCABULARY

Theme-based chapters set a context for learning.

Essential, explicit skills help beginning learners to gain confidence with listening and speaking.

The Grammar Note is matched closely to the listening and speaking tasks for supportive grammar instruction.

Vocabulary is introduced in context and is built from the Oxford 2000 list of keywords.

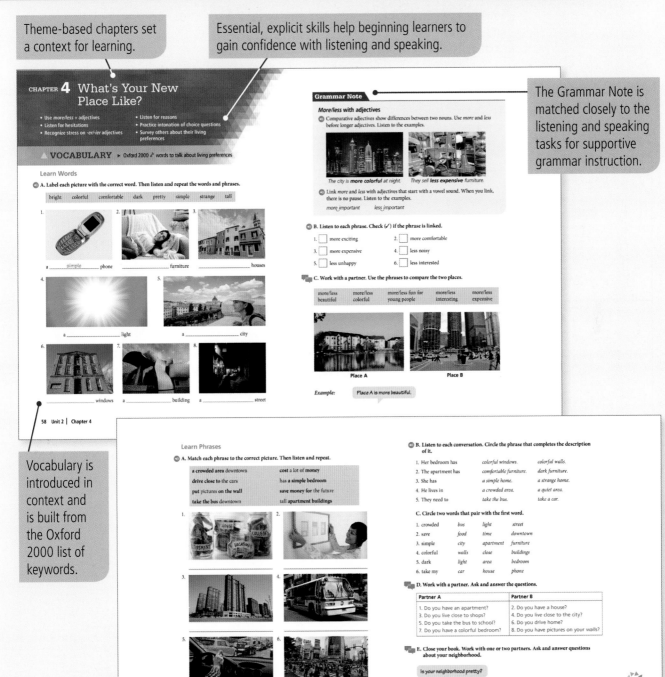

Trio Listening and Speaking Online Practice extends learning beyond the classroom, providing students with additional practice and support for each chapter's vocabulary, grammar, and skills instruction.

Sounds of English boxes provide sound-symbol decoding practice, and link fluency with listening and speaking skills to improve students' understanding of how English is really spoken.

Vocabulary and Grammar Chants found online help students internalize the target grammar structure and vocabulary for greater fluency when listening and speaking.

Conversation activities help students practice words, phrases, and grammar used in everyday situations.

Academic Listening prepares students for academic life.

Listening Strategies give students the techniques they need to listen effectively.

▲▲ LISTENING

CONVERSATION

A. Listen to the conversation. Circle where Hilary wants to live.

outside the city   close to town   downtown

B. Listen to the conversation again. Circle the correct answer.

1. Hilary needs   two   three   bedrooms.
2. She prefers   newer   older   apartments.
3. She wants a place with   lighter   darker   rooms.

Listening Strategy

Listening for hesitations

Speakers use hesitation words like *well*, *so*, and *umm* to say that they need time to think. After hesitation words, speakers usually take a pause. Listen to the examples.

A: **So**...are you my new neighbor?
B: **Umm**...I think so. I'm in Apartment 11.
A: **Well**...then we are neighbors! I'm in Apartment 12.

GO ONLINE for more practice

C. Listen to the parts of the conversation again. Check (✓) the hesitation expression you hear.

1. ✓ well...   ☐ so...   2. ☐ so...   ☐ umm...
3. ☐ so...   ☐ well...   4. ☐ well...   ☐ umm...

D. Practice the conversations with a partner. Then switch roles.

1. A: So...are you in college?   2. A: Is Jackson Street close to here?
    B: Well...no. But I will be next year.   B: Umm...I'm not sure.
3. A: This apartment is really small!   4. A: So...do you want to go eat?
    B: Well...at least it's downtown, right?   B: Well...I'm not really hungry now.
5. A: Why is this area so popular?   6. A: When do you want to meet?
    B: Well...it has the best restaurants.   B: Umm...How about 7?

Sounds of English

Stress on -er/-ier adjectives

For one-syllable adjectives, -er is added to an adjective to show comparison. Comparative adjectives with -er have two syllables. The stress is on the first syllable. Listen to the examples.

small → sm**a**ller   cheap → ch**ea**per

For two-syllable adjectives that end in -y, -ier is used to show comparison. Comparative adjectives with -ier have three syllables. The stress is on the first syllable. Listen to the examples.

pretty → pr**e**ttier   noisy → n**oi**sier

Some comparative adjectives change to new words. Listen to the examples.

good → better   bad → worse

E. Listen to each word and phrase. Check (✓) the phrase you hear.

	A		B
1.	☐ a cheap apartment	✓	a cheaper apartment
2.	☐ a nice café	☐	a nicer café
3.	☐ bright bedrooms	☐	brighter bedrooms
4.	☐ a pretty street	☐	a prettier street
5.	☐ a quiet place	☐	a quieter place

F. Work with a partner. Use the comparative adjectives in the box to compare the two pictures.

better   brighter   darker   noisier   older   prettier   quieter   smaller

Street A   Street B

Chant
GO ONLINE for the Chapter 4 Vocabulary & Grammar Chant

ACADEMIC LISTENING

A. Check (✓) the things you prefer in a home. Share your ideas with a partner.

1. ☐ being in a quiet area   ☐ being in a fun area
2. ☐ living in the city   ☐ living outside the city
3. ☐ being closer to shops   ☐ being closer to nature

B. Listen to the first section of the interview. Circle the correct answer.

1. The interview is about   a new book.   a new movie.
2. Micro apartments are   very small.   very big.
3. Micro apartments have furniture   in the rooms.   in the walls.

C. Listen to the second section of the interview. Complete the statements with *more* or *less* to make them true.

1. People spend _____ money on micro apartments.
2. Living downtown is _____ fun.
3. People have _____ things to do downtown.
4. There are _____ restaurants.
5. There are _____ places to shop.

Listening Strategy

Listening for reasons

Speakers give reasons to explain their ideas. Reasons answer the question *Why?* To introduce a reason, speakers often say *because*. Listen to the example.

A: Why do people want micro apartments?
      reason
B: Well, **because** they're cheaper.

Speakers can use other phrases to explain a reason.
It's also because they're cheaper.
Another reason is that they're cheaper.

GO ONLINE for more practice

D. Listen and match the phrase to the correct statement.

Another reason is that	It's fun because	It's also because

1. _____ micro apartments are downtown.
2. _____ people live closer to everything.
3. _____ downtown is popular.

E. Listen to the interview again. Ask and answer the questions with a partner.

Partner A	Partner B
1. What is a micro apartment?	2. Where do people find micro apartments?
3. Why do people want to live downtown?	4. Why do people like to walk to places?
5. Why do people want micro apartments?	6. What is another reason?

Discuss the Ideas

F. Read the statements. Circle your opinion.

1. It's better to live   in a smaller apartment   in a bigger apartment.
2. It's better to live   in the center of the city.   outside the city.
3. Micro apartments   are good for my city.   are not good for my city.
4. Micro apartments are better for   younger people   older people.

G. Work with a partner. Partner A shares an opinion from Activity F. Partner B asks *Why?* Partner A give a reason with *because*. Then partners switch roles.

It's better to live in a bigger apartment.

Why?

Because you have more space.

▲▲▲ SPEAKING

The Pronunciation Skill helps students to speak clearly and intelligibly.

Carefully staged speaking tasks build student confidence.

Speaking Skills boxes provide explanations of expressions frequently used in spoken English to improve students' natural-sounding speech.

Students discuss a question in small groups to develop critical thinking skills.

▲▲▲ SPEAKING

Speaking Task
Surveying others about their living preferences

Step 1 PREPARE

Pronunciation Skill

Intonation of choice questions

Speakers use *Do you like...?* and *Do you prefer...?* to ask about what people like.

Do you like history?   **Do you prefer** bigger cities?

Speakers use *or* to give people a choice. When you ask choice questions, use rising and falling intonation. Listen to the examples.

A: Do you like history **or** art?   A: Do you prefer bigger **or** smaller cities?
B: I like history.   B: I prefer smaller cities.

GO ONLINE for more practice

A. Listen and repeat.

A	B
1. Do you like soccer?	Do you like soccer or football?
2. Do you like books?	Do you like books or movies?
3. Do you like computers?	Do you like computers or art?
4. Do you prefer coffee?	Do you prefer coffee or tea?
5. Do you prefer old furniture?	Do you prefer old or new furniture?
6. Do you prefer driving to places?	Do you prefer driving or walking to places?

B. Work with a partner. Partner A asks a question from Activity A. Partner B answers the question. Then partners switch roles.

C. Listen to the questions. Check (✓) the best answer.

Yes/no answers	Choice answers
1. ✓ Yes, I do.	☐ I prefer apartments.
2. ☐ No, I don't.	☐ I prefer brighter bedrooms.
3. ☐ Yes, I do.	☐ I like spending money.
4. ☐ Yes, I do.	☐ I prefer quiet streets.
5. ☐ No, I don't.	☐ I like bigger apartments.

D. Work with a partner. Ask and answer the questions with *Do you like...?* or *Do you prefer...?*

Partner A	Partner B
1. ...noisy streets or quiet streets?	2. ...brighter rooms or darker rooms?
3. ...colorful homes or simple homes?	4. ...bigger cities or smaller cities?
5. ...living close to family or to friends?	6. ...being downtown or being in nature?
7. ...friendly or quiet neighbors?	8. ...small stores or big stores?
9. ...taking the bus or driving?	10. ...walking or biking to places?

E. Listen. Complete the conversation with the words from the box.

a little more	drive to school	in class	later	near work

A: So, do you want an apartment near school or _____ near work _____?
B: Umm...that's hard to say.
A: Well, do you spend more time _____ or at work?
B: I spend more time in class. I take four classes.
A: OK. So, apartments near your school are more expensive.
B: So, they cost a lot more or _____?
A: Only a little more, really.
B: That's OK, I guess.
A: OK, and do you bike or _____?
B: Umm...I like to bike. Why?
A: Well, it's a perfect area for bikers. There are lots of places to bike.
B: That sounds great!
A: OK. Let's look at some apartments near school then. Do you want to look now or _____?
B: Let's look now. I have class later.
A: Oh, right. OK, then.

GO ONLINE to practice the conversation

F. Work with a partner. Practice the conversation in Activity E.

66   Unit 2 │ Chapter 4

Step 2 SPEAK

A. Think about the place you want to live. Check (✓) the things you prefer.

☐ living in the city   ☐ living outside the city
☐ older buildings   ☐ newer buildings
☐ a smaller apartment   ☐ a bigger apartment

Speaking Skill

Using *because* to add information

Speakers use *because* to give more information. *Because* often explains why people like or prefer something. Listen to the examples.

I like cities **because** they're fun.
I prefer an apartment **because** it's cheaper.

Speakers often reduce *because* to *'cuz*. It sounds shorter and softer. Listen to the examples.

I like cities **'cuz** they're fun.
I prefer an apartment **'cuz** it's cheaper.

Partners

prefer living
prefer going
prefer doing
prefer having
prefer being

GO ONLINE to practice word partners

I like a bigger place 'cuz I have a lot of furniture.

B. Work with a partner. Use the words in the chart and your own ideas to describe what you like or prefer.

I like / I prefer	a bigger place being close to shops having an apartment living in the city older buildings quieter areas a simpler home	because... 'cuz...

Speaking Task
Surveying classmates about their living preferences

1. Write two more questions in the chart. Then complete the survey about you.

	Me	Partner 1	Partner 2
Do you prefer an apartment or a house?			

2. Close your book. Work with two partners to ask and answer the survey questions.

Step 3 REPORT

Complete the sentences with information from your survey to write a report. Share your findings with the class to learn about popular places to live.

_____ prefers _____.
wants to be close to _____.
does not like _____.
_____ prefers _____.
wants to be close to _____.
does not like _____.

Step 4 REFLECT

Checklist

Check (✓) the things you learned in Chapter 4.

○ I learned language to describe living preferences.
○ I understood an interview about micro apartments.
○ I surveyed and reported on my classmates' living preferences.

Discussion Question

Are micro apartments better for young people?

Speaking   69

68   Unit 2 │ Chapter 4

Trio Listening and Speaking Online Practice: Essential Digital Content

Trio Listening and Speaking Online Practice provides multiple opportunities for skills practice and acquisition—beyond the classroom and beyond the page.

Each unit of ***Trio Listening and Speaking*** is accompanied by a variety of automatically graded activities. Students' progress is recorded, tracked, and fed back to the instructor.

Vocabulary and Grammar Chants help students internalize the target grammar structure and vocabulary for greater accuracy and fluency when listening and speaking.

Online Activities provide essential practice of Vocabulary, Grammar, Listening, Speaking, and Pronunication.

GO ONLINE icons lead students to essential digital content.

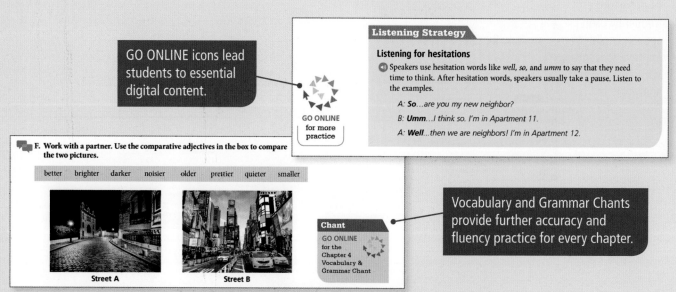

Vocabulary and Grammar Chants provide further accuracy and fluency practice for every chapter.

Use the access code on the inside front cover to log in at **www.oxfordlearn.com/login**.

Readiness Unit

Vocabulary

Letters, words, and sentences
Numbers
Verbs
Nouns
Adjectives
Phrases

Listening

Syllables in words
Stress
Intonation
Wh- questions
Repetition

Speaking

Pronouns
Short answers
Everyday expressions

UNIT WRAP UP Extend Your Skills

Letters, words, and sentences

◀)) The English alphabet has 26 letters. Letters are CAPITAL and lowercase. Listen to the alphabet.

CAPITAL:

A B C D E F G H I J K L M N O P Q R S T U V W X Y Z

lowercase:

a b c d e f g h i j k l m n o p q r s t u v w x y z

◀)) **A. Circle the two letters you hear.**

1. A B C   2. D E F   3. G H I   4. J K L

5. M N O   6. P Q R   7. S T U V   8. W X Y Z

◀)) **B. Listen again and check your answers in Activity A.**

Letters form words. Words form sentences.

◀)) **C. Listen to the letters. Then listen to the words. Then listen to the sentence.**

Letters	a m	n e w	s t u d e n t
Words	am	new	student
Sentence	I am a new student.		

Numbers

◀)) Numbers tell how many. Listen to the numbers.

1 one	2 two	3 three	4 four	5 five
6 six	7 seven	8 eight	9 nine	10 ten

◀)) **A. Circle the numbers you hear.**

1 2 3 4 5 6 7 8 9 10

◀)) **B. Listen again and check your answers in Activity A.**

Verbs

VERBS IN THE CLASSROOM

🔊 Many verbs describe classroom directions. Look at the pictures, read the verbs, and listen to the directions.

work with a partner

say the words

2. What hides beneath
3. We _play_ games.
4. He _____ the park.
5. The teacher _____ the bo
6. _____ is the best sport.

write the answer

read the directions

ask a question

answer a question

practice in groups

ENGLISH _a_ a. book b. computer

match the picture to the word

repeat the word

🔊 **A. Circle the words to complete the verb phrase. Then listen and check your answers.**

1. listen to (your teacher) the classroom   2. practice   in groups   the directions
3. answer   the questions   a conversation   4. work   the words   with a partner
5. read   the people   the answer   6. say   the letter   a check
7. circle   the letter   a partner   8. match   the pictures the classrooms
9. write   the words   a game   10. repeat   the question the circle

VERBS THAT DESCRIBE ACTIONS

Some verbs describe actions. Look at the pictures and listen to the action verbs.

study English   *live* in a city   *play* games

see a friend   *eat* food   *go* home

VERBS THAT GIVE INFORMATION

Some verbs give information and ideas. Look at the pictures and listen to the non-action verbs.

like sports   *have* a phone   *be* a student

B. Listen to the word and the phrase. Circle the verb you hear.

1. (have)   put
2. read   learn
3. eat   work
4. answer   practice
5. write   say
6. listen   repeat
7. match   listen
8. be   go

Nouns

🔊 Some words are nouns. Nouns are people, places, and things. Listen and repeat the nouns.

People

man

woman

friends

Places

a city

a store

a park

Things

food

a game

sports

🔊 **A. Look at the pictures. Listen to the classroom nouns.**

a computer

a teacher

a book

information

a classroom

a school

🔊 **B. Match each sentence to the correct picture. Then listen and check your answers.**

4 **Friends** play **sports** at a **park**.

8 **Partners** have a **conversation**.

2 **People** buy **books** at **stores**.

1 A **teacher** uses a **computer** at **school**.

5 **Men** eat **food** in the **city**.

6 **Women** get **information** from **books**.

3 A **student** has an **idea** at **home**.

7 A **woman** plays a **game** on her **phone**.

1.
2.
3.
4.
5.
6.
7.
8.

C. Use a noun to complete each sentence about yourself. Share your sentences with a partner.

1. I have _____

2. I like _____

3. I use _____

Adjectives

Adjectives describe nouns. Listen and repeat the adjectives.

an **expensive** computer

a **smiling** woman

a **big** campus

a **beautiful** park

an **important** man

a **good** friend

similar phones

different phones

a **small** store

new clothes

A. Circle the correct adjective to describe each noun. Then listen and check your answers.

1. a (small) new book

2. a new similar (home)

3. a happy different (student)

4. an important early (school)

5. a similar big (friend)

6. a beautiful tall (park)

7. a big happy (computer)

8. a (different) small color

9. an expensive angry (sport)

10. a good short (idea)

Phrases

Phrases are groups of words that work together. Two common types of phrases are noun phrases and verb phrases.

Noun phrases	Verb phrases
a computer a big city an important book my friend	answer the question eat good food go home work in groups

 A. Listen and match the words to create noun phrases.

1. a. a happy   friend
   b. a good   teacher
   c. a new   partner

      I have a good friend.

      You have a good friend.

2. a. a big   computer
   b. an expensive   phone
   c. a different   book

3. a. a similar   home
   b. a new   city
   c. a beautiful   school

B. Work with a partner. Partner A says a phrase with *I have*. Partner B repeats the phrase with *You have*. Then partners switch roles.

 C. Listen and match the words to make verb phrases.

1. a. read   words
   b. write   books
   c. use   ideas

      I read books.

      You read books.

2. a. learn about   new cities
   b. like   different schools
   c. see   beautiful homes

3. a. live near   expensive stores
   b. have   a nice park
   c. go to   good schools

 D. Work with a partner. Partner A says a phrase with *I*. Partner B repeats the phrase with *You*.

Syllables in words

🔊 Some words have one sound called a syllable. Other words have two, three, or more syllables. Usually one or more syllables is louder or stronger. Listen to the examples.

One syllable:	*class*	*big*	*read*
Two syllables:	**stu•**dent	**hap•**py	**prac•**tice
Three syllables:	com•**pu•**ter	**beau•**ti•ful	im•**por•**tant

🔊 **A. Listen to each word. Write *1, 2, 3,* or *4* for the number of syllables you hear.**

1. have ___1___   2. sports _____

3. important _____   4. expensive _____

5. good _____   6. classroom _____

7. conversation _____   8. information _____

9. people _____   10. circle _____

🔊 **B. Listen to the words in Activity A again. Practice saying the words.**

Stress

In phrases and sentences, English words follow a stress pattern. Nouns, verbs, and adjectives are louder and stronger. This is called *sentence stress*.

🔊 Small words such as *a, an, the, my, some, to, in, and,* and *at* are usually not stressed in phrases and sentences. Listen to the examples.

a **book**	read a **book** in **class**
the **words**	**listen** to the **words** and **phrases**
some **food**	**eat** some **food**
my **phone**	**see** my **new phone**

🔊 **A. Listen and repeat the phrases.**

1. like	**like** a **city**	**like** a **big city**
2. play	**play** on a com**pu**ter	**play** on a **small** com**pu**ter
3. listen	**lis**ten to my i**dea**	**lis**ten to my **great** i**dea**
4. say	**say** the **words**	**say** the **new words**
5. talk	**talk** to a **part**ner	**talk** to a **different part**ner
6. go	**go** to the **lib**rary	**go** to the **school lib**rary

◆ B. Listen and put a check (✓) next to the phrase you hear.

A	B
1. [✓] have a fun partner	[ ] have a good teacher
2. [ ] find a good book	[ ] find a new park
3. [ ] listen to your partner's words	[ ] listen for the new verbs
4. [ ] see a big city	[ ] see a new student
5. [ ] listen and repeat	[ ] listen and then read

C. Work with a partner. Partner A says *I* and a phrase from Activity B. Partner B says the letter of the phrase. Then partners switch roles.

Intonation

◆ *Yes/no* questions have a rising intonation. The voice goes up (↗). Statements have falling intonation. The voice goes down (↘). Listen to the examples.

Question ↗	**Statement ↘**
Do you have a phone?	You have a phone.
Does your teacher explain ideas?	My teacher explains ideas.

◆ A. Listen and put a check (✓) next to the question or sentence you hear.

Yes/no questions	Statements
1. [ ] Are you a student?	[ ] You are a student.
2. [ ] Are you new?	[ ] You are new.
3. [ ] Do you have a phone?	[ ] You have a phone.
4. [ ] Do you like your computer?	[ ] You like your computer.
5. [ ] Is it expensive?	[ ] It is expensive.
6. [ ] Is it small?	[ ] It is small.

B. Work with a partner. Partner A says a question or sentence from Activity A. Partner B points to the correct sentence or question. Then partners switch roles.

Wh- questions

Information questions begin with *wh-* words, such as *who?*, *what?*, *when?*, and *where?*

Wh- word	Information question	Statement
who for people	Who is your partner?	My partner is Michel.
what for things /ideas	What do you study?	I study English.
when for time	When do you study?	I study after dinner.
where for places	Where do you study?	I study at home.

Information questions and sentences usually have a falling intonation (⌒). Listen to the examples.

⌒ What do you have? ⌒ I have a book.

⌒ Where do you live? ⌒ I live near school.

A. Listen to each question and answer. Check (✓) the question you hear.

A

1. ☐ What is...?
2. ☐ Who is...?
3. ☐ When is...?
4. ☐ Where is...?
5. ☐ Who is...?

B

☐ When do...?
☐ Where do...?
☐ What does...?
☐ When do...?
☐ Who does...?

B. Listen and repeat.

Information questions

1. What is your name?
2. What is this class?
3. Where do you go?
4. Who do you see?
5. Who do you like?

Statements

My name is Sam.

This class is math.

I go to school.

I see my teacher.

I like my new friend.

C. Work with a partner. Partner A asks a question from Activity B. Partner B says the response. Then partners switch roles.

Repetition

🔊 Speakers repeat the topic two, three, or more times. Listen to the example about books. The speaker uses the word *books* three times.

> Books are important. Students read five or six books a semester. Many students use computers now, but they still use books.

🔊 **A. Listen to each talk. Write the topic from the box in the chart. Then listen again. Write the number of times you hear the topic.**

cities	computers	food

Topic	Number of times you hear topic
1.	
2.	
3.	

🔊 **B. Listen to the talks again. Put a check (✓) when you hear an idea.**

1. Cities are big.

a. ☐ Many people live in cities.

b. ☐ They are similar in some ways.

c. ☐ They all have schools and homes.

d. ☐ They all have parks.

e. ☐ Every city is different, too.

2. People like good food.

a. ☐ Today we will talk about expensive food.

b. ☐ Expensive food is beautiful.

c. ☐ People eat it in restaurants.

d. ☐ Some good food is not expensive.

3. Computers are important.

a. ☐ You use computers at school.

b. ☐ There are many different kinds of computers.

c. ☐ Your phone is a small computer.

d. ☐ There are many different computers in your home.

Pronouns

🔊 When speakers answer questions, they often use pronouns. Pronouns replace subjects. Listen to the examples.

A: What does **your teacher** do?
B: **She** explains ideas.

A: What do the **men and women** do?
B: **They** play sports.

A: Is **the book** good?
B: Yes, **it** is great!

A: What do **you** play?
B: **I** play soccer.

🔊 **A. Match each answer to the correct question. Then listen and check your answers.**

1. Where is she?   ___f___   a. They're my friends.

2. Who are they?   _____   b. Yes, I am good at sports.

3. How is the food?   _____   c. Yes, we are similar.

4. Who is that man?   _____   d. He's new at school.

5. Are you good at sports? _____   e. It is good.

6. Are you and I similar?   _____   f. She's at home.

B. Work with a partner. Partner A asks a question. Partner B answers with a statement. Then partners switch roles.

Information questions	Statements
1. Where is she? Where is he?	She's at school. He's at home.
2. Where do students go? Where do you go?	They go to school. I go to school.
3. Is the food good? Is the student new?	Yes, it is good. Yes, he is new.
4. What does he see? What do people like?	He sees a beautiful park. They like beautiful places.

Short answers

Speakers often answer *yes/no* questions with short answers. Listen to the examples.

Yes/no questions	Short answers	
Are you a student?	Yes, I am.	No, I'm not.
Are we in different classes?	Yes, we are.	No, we're not.
Is it good?	Yes, it is.	No, it's not.
Is he a teacher?	Yes, he is.	No, he's not.

A. Read the questions. Write a short answer about you. Then practice the conversations with a partner.

1. A: Are you good at sports?
   B: _____

2. A: Is your teacher nice?
   B: _____

3. A: Are your friends similar?
   B: _____

4. A: Is your phone important to you?
   B: _____

Speakers often answer information questions quickly with words and short phrases. Listen to the examples.

Information questions	Answers
What is your name?	Tran.
Who is your partner?	Rodolfo.
Where do you live?	Near school.
What does she use?	A phone.

B. Read the questions. Write a short answer about you. Then practice the conversations with a partner.

1. A: What is your name?

   B: _____

2. A: Where do you live?

   B: _____

3. A: Who is your partner?

   B: _____

4. A: What do you like?

   B: _____

Everyday expressions

In conversations, people use sentences, questions, and short answers. Read and listen to the example.

A. Look at the pictures and listen to the conversations.

A: How are you?
B: I'm fine, and you?

A: I like your phone.
B: Thanks. It's new.

A: Is it important?
B: I'm not sure. Maybe.
A: OK, I'll answer it.

A: This is my computer.
B: Wow! Is it new?
A: Yes!

 B. Practice the conversations in Activity A with a partner.

C. Match each statement and question with the correct short answer. Then listen and check your answers.

1. a. This is my home.
   b. Do you like my new computer?

   ___b___ Yes. It looks expensive!
   ___a___ Wow! It's beautiful.

2. a. Is your friend at home?
   b. Do you have the answer?

   _____ Maybe. Let's ask the teacher.
   _____ I'm not sure.

3. a. I have a book for you.
   b. How are you?

   _____ I'm fine.
   _____ Great! Thank you.

4. a. Do you have a class now?
   b. Is the class important?

   _____ Yes, I have to go.
   _____ Maybe. I am not sure.

D. Work with a partner. Practice the conversations in Activity C.

E. Listen to each conversation and write the correct word or phrase from the box.

~~Maybe.~~   Wow!

1. A: Do you know her?   B: _____Maybe._____ I'm not sure.

great   now

2. A: Do you have a class later?   B: No, _____. Bye!

Great!   Please.

3. A: The students are happy.   B: _____

Wow!   Thank you.

4. A: Look at that park!   B: _____ It's beautiful.

later   OK

5. A: Do you want some food?   B: No, not now. Maybe _____.

Oh.   I'm fine.

6. A: How are you?   B: _____ How are you?

F. Work with a partner. Practice the conversations in Activity E.

Look at the word bank for the Readiness Unit. Check (✓) the words you know. Circle the words you want to learn better.

OXFORD 2000 🔑				
Adjectives	**Nouns**		**Verbs**	
beautiful	book	park	answer	match
big	city	partner	ask	play
correct	computer	phone	be	practice
different	conversation	picture	check	read
expensive	food	question	circle	repeat
good	friend	school	eat	say
happy	game	sport	go	see
important	group	store	have	study
new	home	student	like	work
similar	idea	teacher	listen	write
small	information	woman	live	
	man	word		
	number			

PRACTICE WITH THE OXFORD 2000 🔑

A. Use the chart. Match adjectives with nouns.

1. _____a new phone_____   2. _____

3. _____   4. _____

5. _____   6. _____

B. Use the chart. Match verbs with nouns.

1. _____see a city_____   2. _____

3. _____   4. _____

5. _____   6. _____

C. Use the chart. Match verbs with adjective noun partners.

1. _____ask a good question_____   2. _____

3. _____   4. _____

5. _____   6. _____

UNIT **1** People

CHAPTER **1** — Are You Ready?

▲ **VOCABULARY** — • Oxford 2000 🔑 words to talk about school

▲▲ **LISTENING**
- Listening for questions and statements
- Listening for directions

▲▲▲ **SPEAKING**
- Practicing stress on two-syllable adjectives
- Making small talk with new classmates

CHAPTER **2** — Do You Like Music?

▲ **VOCABULARY** — • Oxford 2000 🔑 words to talk about interests

▲▲ **LISTENING**
- Listening to learn about activities people like
- Listening for a speaker's questions

▲▲▲ **SPEAKING**
- Practicing stress on nouns
- Sharing interests with others

CHAPTER **3** — Do You Want to Meet for Coffee?

▲ **VOCABULARY**
- Oxford 2000 🔑 words to talk about places on campus

▲▲ **LISTENING**
- Listening for *here* and *there*
- Listening for sequence words

▲▲▲ **SPEAKING**
- Practicing linking with the schwa /ə/ sound
- Making plans to get together with classmates

UNIT WRAP UP — Extend Your Skills

CHAPTER 1 Are You Ready?

- Use *are you?* and *I am* with adjectives
- Listen for questions and statements
- Recognize the reduction of *do you*
- Listen for directions
- Practice stress on two-syllable adjectives
- Make small talk with new classmates

▲ VOCABULARY ▶ Oxford 2000 🔑 words to talk about school

Learn Words

🔊 **A. Label each picture with the correct word. Then listen and repeat the words and phrases.**

busy	confused	friendly	fun	helpful	~~nervous~~	noisy	quiet

1.

a _____nervous_____ parent

2.

a _Friendly_ teacher

3.

a _Fun_ class

4.

a _____ student

5.

a _____ counselor

6.

a _____ night

7.

a _____ place

8.

_____ children

Grammar Note

Are you? and *I am* with adjectives

Speakers use *are you?* and *I am* with adjectives to ask and answer questions about feelings. *I am* becomes *I'm* in spoken English. Listen to the examples.

Question	Answer	Short answer	Negative short answer
Are you ready? →	Yes, **I'm** ready.	Yes, **I am**.	No, **I'm** not.
Are you nervous? →	Yes, **I'm** nervous.	Yes, **I am**.	No, **I'm** not.

B. Listen and repeat.

1. Are you ready?   Yes, I'm ready.
2. Are you nervous?   Yes, I'm nervous.
3. Are you busy?   Yes, I'm busy.
4. Are you happy?   Yes, I'm happy.
5. Are you confused?   Yes, I'm confused.
6. Are you quiet?   Yes, I'm quiet.

C. Work with a partner. Ask and answer the questions in Activity B.

D. Listen to each question. Check (✓) the answer you hear.

Question	*Yes* answer	*No* answer
1. Are you confused?	✓ Yes, I am.	☐ No, I'm not.
2. Are you ready?	☐ Yes, I am.	☐ No, I'm not.
3. Are you busy?	☐ Yes, I am.	☐ No, I'm not.
4. Are you quiet?	☐ Yes, I am.	☐ No, I'm not.
5. Are you nervous?	☐ Yes, I am.	☐ No, I'm not.
6. Are you happy?	☐ Yes, I am.	☐ No, I'm not.

E. Work with a partner. Partner A asks each question in Activity D. Partner B answers with a *yes* or *no* answer. Partner A points to the answer given. Then partners switch roles.

Learn Phrases

A. Match each phrase to the correct picture. Then listen and repeat.

5	**a great place** to study with classmates	1	everybody **raise your hand**
6	**find a good time** to meet today	2	**get to know** your teacher
8	**have fun** at the park	3	**look around** the bookstore
4	**work hard** on the computer	7	**worry about** my homework

1.

2.

3.

4.

5.

6.

7.

8.

B. Listen to the speakers. Check (✓) the sentence or phrase you hear.

1. ☐	Don't worry about your teacher.	✓	Don't worry about the papers.
2. ☐	Everybody is in class.	✓	Everybody has a book.
3. ✓	Look around the park.	☐	Look around the school.
4. ✓	a good time to meet	☐	a good time to eat
5. ✓	have fun at home	☐	see friends at home
6. ✓	work hard	☐	walk here

C. Add words to make new phrases.

1. A great place to meet is   the park.

    the library. _____

2. I want to get to know   my partner.

    _____

3. look around   the campus

    _____

4. worry about   my classes

    _____

5. have fun at   a café

    _____

6. find a good time to   do homework

    _____

D. Work with a partner. Ask and answer the questions.

Partner A	Partner B
1. Is the library a good place to meet?	2. Is everybody busy?
3. Do students work hard in this school?	4. Is now a good time to ask questions?
5. Do your classmates have fun in class?	6. Look around the room. Do you see a friend?
7. Is this campus a great place to meet people?	8. Do you worry about your classes?

E. Close your book. Work with one or two partners. Ask and answer questions about the class.

GO ONLINE for more practice

▲▲ LISTENING

CONVERSATION

🔊 **A. Listen to the conversation. Check (✓) the picture that matches the conversation.**

🔊 **B. Listen to the conversation again. Circle two words that describe the student.**

busy   nervous   new

GO ONLINE
for more
practice

Listening Strategy

Listening for questions and statements

🔊 Sometimes people start conversations with a question. Then they respond to the answer with a comment. Listen. Then practice the conversations with a partner.

Question	Answer	Comment
Are you busy? →	*Yes, I am.*	*Yeah, everybody is busy right now.*
Are you nervous? →	*Yes, very!*	*That's OK. All new students are a little nervous today.*
Are you confused? →	*No, not really.*	*That's great.*

🔊 **C. Listen to the conversation again. After you hear each question, circle the answer you hear.**

1. Are you a new student?	*Yes, I am.*	*No, I'm not.*
2. Are you ready for school?	*Yes, I am.*	*No, not really.*
3. Are you nervous?	*Yes, a little*	*No, not at all.*
4. Do you have any questions?	*Yes, I do.*	*No, not right now.*

💬 **D. Work with a partner. Ask the questions in Activity C and answer about yourself. Then switch roles.**

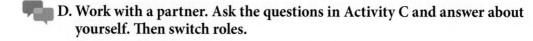

Are you a new student?

Yes, I am.

Reduction of *do you*

When speakers say *do you* quickly, it sometimes sounds like *duya*. Listen to the examples.

> Do you like your teachers? → **Duya** like your teachers?
>
> Do you have your books? → **Duya** have your books?

E. Listen and repeat.

1. Do you like your teachers?	Yes, I do.	No, I don't.
2. Do you feel nervous?	Yes, I do.	No, I don't.
3. Do you have your books?	Yes, I do.	No, I don't.
4. Do you want some help?	Yes, I do.	No, I don't.
5. Do you have a question?	Yes, I do.	No, I don't.
6. Do you meet people in class?	Yes, I do.	No, I don't.

F. Listen to each speaker. Check (✓) the question or statement you hear.

A   **B**

1. [✓] Do you like your classmates?   [ ] I like my classmates.

2. [ ] Do you have good teachers?   [ ] I have good teachers.

3. [ ] Do you feel nervous in class?   [ ] I feel nervous in class.

4. [ ] Do you want some help?   [ ] We want some help.

5. [ ] Do you have fun with friends?   [ ] We have fun with friends.

G. Work with a partner. Partner A says a question or sentence from Activity F. Partner B says the letter of the correct column. Then partners switch roles.

H. Listen to the speakers. Write *Do you* or *Are you* to complete the questions.

1. _____Do you_____ like to meet new people?

2. _____ speak English?

3. _____ ready for class?

4. _____ like your teacher?

5. _____ busy today?

Chant

GO ONLINE for the Chapter 1 Vocabulary & Grammar Chant

ACADEMIC LISTENING

A. **Read each item. Check (✓) the answer that is correct for you. Then compare your answers with a partner. Are you similar or different?**

	Very important	Important	Not important
1. meet new friends			
2. study hard			
3. have helpful teachers			
4. have fun			
5. have a lot of homework			

 B. **Work in a group of three. Take turns asking and answering the questions.**

1. Do you like to practice in groups?

2. Do you ask your classmates for help?

3. Do you study with friends?

C. **Listen to the first section. Circle the correct answer to complete each statement.**

1. The speaker is talking to   *a group of new students.*   *everybody at the school.*

2. The speaker feels   *nervous.*   *happy.*

3. The speaker is talking about   *the college campus.*   *the city.*

D. **Listen to the whole talk. Complete the speaker's questions with the words from the box.**

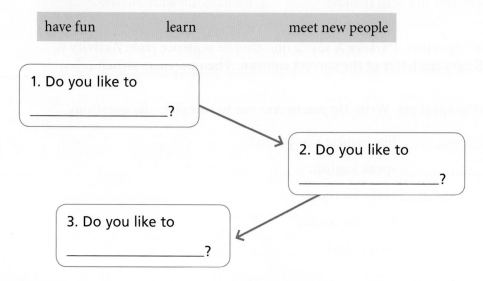

have fun	learn	meet new people

1. Do you like to

_____?

2. Do you like to

_____?

3. Do you like to

_____?

Listening for directions

When speakers talk to classes and big groups, they want to know what their audience thinks. When speakers want ideas from their audience, they give directions.

- They ask their audience an information question.
- They ask their audience to raise their hands to show *yes* or *no*.
- They ask their audience to talk to a partner.

GO ONLINE
for more practice

 E. Listen to the talk again. Check (✓) the strategies you hear.

☐ 1. The speaker asks the students to answer an information question.

☐ 2. The speaker asks the students to raise their hands to show *yes*.

☐ 3. The speaker asks the students to raise their hands to show *no*.

☐ 4. The speaker asks the students to talk to a partner.

F. Work with a partner. Ask and answer the questions.

Partner A	Partner B
1. Is the speaker friendly?	2. Does the speaker like Cedars College?
3. Do students want to meet new friends?	4. Do students have fun on campus?
5. Are the students happy?	6. Are the students ready to have fun?

Discuss the Ideas

 G. Work in a group. Partner A reads a question and a direction from the box. Partners B and C listen and follow the direction. Then partners switch roles.

Question	Direction
Do you like to learn? Do you play sports? Do you like your teachers? Do you read books? Do you speak English? Do you like to have fun?	Raise your hand. Tell a partner.

▲▲▲ SPEAKING

Speaking Task Making small talk with new classmates

Step 1 PREPARE

Pronunciation Skill

Stress on two-syllable adjectives

🔊 Most two-syllable adjectives have the stress on the first syllable. Listen to the adjectives alone, in a question, and in a sentence.

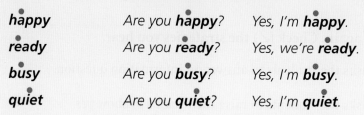

happy	Are you **happy**?	Yes, I'm **happy**.
ready	Are you **ready**?	Yes, we're **ready**.
busy	Are you **busy**?	Yes, I'm **busy**.
quiet	Are you **quiet**?	Yes, I'm **quiet**.

Note: The adjective *confused* has a stress on the second syllable: *confused*

GO ONLINE
for more
practice

🔊 **A. Listen and repeat.**

1. happy   I'm happy.

2. busy   We're busy.

3. nervous   I'm nervous.

4. helpful   You're helpful.

🔊 **B. Listen and repeat each question and answer.**

1. Are you busy?   Yes, I'm busy, very busy.

2. Are you nervous?   Yes, I'm nervous, very nervous.

3. Are you friendly?   Yes, I'm friendly, very friendly.

4. Are you happy?   Yes, I'm happy, very happy.

5. Are you worried?   Yes, I'm worried, very worried.

💬 **C. Work with a partner. Ask and answer the questions in Activity B.**

🔊 **D. Listen to the conversation and write the words you hear. Then practice with a partner.**

Speaker 1	Speaker 2	Speaker 1
1. I'm _____ with school.	Happy?	No, _____ !
2. I'm _____ about my classes.	Worried?	No, _____ !
3. I'm _____ in class.	Noisy?	No, _____ !

E. Listen. Complete the conversation with the words from the box.

confused	different	friendly	helpful	noisy	~~quiet~~	worried

Ana: Do you need a _____quiet_____ place to study?

Midori: Yes, I do. I am _____ about my class.

Ana: Me, too! The teacher is nice, but I don't understand everything.

Midori: I know, right? The teachers are all _____, but it's hard to understand sometimes.

Ana: Yeah! Sometimes, I am _____, too.

Midori: You get confused? Really?

Ana: Yes!

Midori: Oh, good, it's not just me!

Ana: Everybody gets confused sometimes, but the teachers are _____. They answer questions.

Midori: Well, this place is _____. We need to find a _____ place to study.

Ana: OK, how about the library?

Midori: Sounds good. Let's go.

GO ONLINE
to practice the conversation

 F. Work with a partner. Practice the conversation in Activity E.

 G. Work with a partner. Partner A asks a question. Partner B answers correctly. Then partners switch roles.

1. a. Are they noisy?   Yes, they are.
   b. They have noisy friends.   Uh huh, they do.

2. a. Are you ready for school?   Yes, I'm ready.
   b. I'm ready for school.   Good for you!

3. a. Do you have helpful teachers?   Yes, I do. They're very helpful.
   b. Do you help your teachers?   Not a lot. They help me.

4. a. Are they busy today?   Yes, they are.
   b. They're busy today.   I know, very busy.

5. a. Do you meet friendly people at school?   Yes. My classmates are great.
   b. Are you friendly to people at school?   Yes, I am.

6. a. They're busy with sports.   Yes, they play a lot.
   b. We're busy with sports.   Yes, we are.

Step 2 SPEAK

A. Complete the sentences with information about you.

1. I am a(n) _____ person.

2. I feel _____ today.

3. People in my class are _____.

4. I think this class is _____.

Speaking Skill

Making small talk

🔊 Ask a friendly question to make small talk with a new person. Listen to the examples.

> *Are you ready for class?*
>
> *Are you new to campus?*
>
> *Are you a student here?*

After the person answers, you can continue the conversation by sharing about yourself or repeating the person's answer to show interest.

 B. Work with a partner. Use the words in the chart and your own ideas to practice a conversation.

Speaker 1		Speaker 2	Speaker 1
Are you ready for	class? school?	Yes, I think so. Well, I'm nervous.	That's good. I understand.
Do you like your	book? campus?	Yes, it's interesting. It's OK.	I'm happy to hear that. Oh, really?

Are you ready for school?

Yes, I think so.

Really? Well, I'm worried.

Oh, really?

Word Partners

ready to learn

ready for class

ready to meet people

ready for fun

ready to work

ready for school

GO ONLINE
to practice
word partners

Speaking Task

Making small talk with new classmates

1. Complete the questions and answers. Then practice with a partner.

Questions

1. Are you ready for _____?

2. Do you like _____?

3. How do you feel about _____?

Answers

1. Right now, I feel _____.

2. I like _____.

3. Well, I'm happy about _____.

2. Close your book. Walk around the room. When your teacher says to stop, look for a partner. Ask a question and answer a question.

3. When your teacher says to go, walk around and find a new partner.

Step 3 REPORT

Circle the words to complete the sentences. Use the sentences to write a report.

1. My classmates are   *friendly*   *confused*   *nervous*   *busy*.

2. School is   *important*   *not important*   to them.

3. They like   *the campus*   *computers*   *sports*   *their classmates*   *their teachers*.

Step 4 REFLECT

Checklist

Check (✓) the things you learned in Chapter 1.

○ I learned words and phrases for talking about school.

○ I understood a speaker talking about campus life.

○ I made small talk with my classmates.

Discussion Question

What do students like about campus life?

CHAPTER 2 Do You Like Music?

- Use *wh-* words with *do you*
- Listen to learn about activities people like
- Recognize contractions with *not*
- Listen for a speaker's questions
- Practice stress on nouns
- Share interests with others

▲ VOCABULARY ▶ Oxford 2000 ✐ words to talk about interests

Learn Words

🔊 **A. Label each picture with the correct word. Then listen and repeat the words and phrases.**

beaches	clothes	movies	music	restaurants	teams	technology	walks

1.
exciting _____ *movies* _____

2.
beautiful _____ *beaches* _____

3.
special _____ *clothes* _____

4.
sports _____ *teams* _____

5.
nature _____ *walks* _____

6.
new _____ *technology* _____

7.
interesting _____ *restaurants* _____

8.
popular _____ *Music* _____

Grammar Note

Wh- words with *do you*

To ask for information about other people: Use *What do you...?* for things and activities, use *Who do you..?* for people, and use *Where do you...?* for places.

> **What do you** like? → *movies*
>
> **Who do you** go with? → *my friends*
>
> **Where do you** go? → *downtown*

B. Write *What*, *Who*, or *Where* to complete each question. Then listen and check your answers.

1. ____what____ do you do on the weekend? —— play soccer
2. ____Who____ do you like? —— my friends
3. ____what____ do you want? —— nice clothes
4. ____Where____ do you meet? —— at the gym
5. ____Where____ do you go? —— to the park
6. ____What____ do you talk about? —— movies

C. Work with a partner. Ask and answer the questions in Activity B.

D. Listen. Check (✓) the question you hear. Circle the correct answer.

A	B	A
1. ☐ Who do you like?	✓ What do you like?	(beautiful music) my friend
2. ☐ What do you want?	☐ Where do you go?	expensive restaurants new clothes
3. ☐ Where do you meet?	☐ Who do you see?	my partner at the beach
4. ☐ Who do you like?	☐ What do you have?	a phone friendly people
5. ☐ What do you play?	☐ Where do you play?	at a park soccer
6. ☐ Where do you meet?	☐ Who do you talk to?	downtown my friend

E. Work with a partner. Partner A asks each question from Activity D. Partner B says the correct answer. Then partners switch roles.

Learn Phrases

🔊 **A. Match each phrase to the correct picture. Then listen and repeat.**

exercise **at the gym**	**get together** with friends
go downtown and have lunch	**go shopping** on the weekend
go swimming at the beach	**join a** book **club**
relax in nature together	**watch a movie** at a theater

1.

get together

2.

relax in nature

3.

watch a movie

4.

go shopping

5.

go swimming

6.

at the gym

7.

go downtown

8.

join a book club

B. Listen to each conversation. Check (✓) the phrase you hear.

1. ✓ play computer games   ☐ eat in restaurants

2. ☐ listen to music   ☐ go to school

3. ☐ go shopping   ☐ take nature walks

4. ☐ eat good food   ☐ go to the movies

5. ☐ go swimming   ☐ play soccer

6. ☐ stay home   ☐ go to the gym

C. Read each question. Check (✓) the answer that is correct for you. Then work with a partner. Ask and answer the questions.

	In nature	Downtown	At school	At home
1. Where do you take walks?				
2. Where do you listen to music?				
3. Where do you exercise?				
4. Where do you get together with friends?				
5. Where do you watch movies?				
6. Where do you eat?				

D. Work with a partner. Take turns asking and answering the questions.

1. Do you like movies?
   What movie do you like?

2. Do you like shopping?
   Where do you go shopping for clothes?

3. Do you like sports?
   Who do you play with?

4. Do you like good restaurants?
   What restaurant do you like?

5. Do you like nature?
   Where do you see nature?

6. Do you like music?
   What kind of music do you like?

Do you like music?

Yes, I do.

What kind of music do you like?

Pop music.

GO ONLINE for more practice

E. Close your book. Work with one or two partners. Ask and answer questions about things you like.

▲▲ LISTENING

CONVERSATION

🔊 **A. Listen to the conversation. Circle the correct answers.**

1. Where are the students?   *downtown*   *at a park*   *in class*

2. What is the topic?   *cities*   *the campus*   *weekend activities*

3. Who is Kamyar?   *a teacher*   *a student*   *a counselor*

🔊 **B. Listen to the conversation again. Check (✓) what each student likes.**

	Shopping for clothes	Listening to music	Swimming at the beach	Watching movies
Kamyar				
Jun				
Maria				
Kurt				

GO ONLINE
for more
practice

Listening Strategy

Listening to learn about activities people like

🔊 People often use *like* with verb + *ing* to describe activities they like. Listen to the examples.

I like watching movies.   *Maria likes shopping.*   *Kurt likes listening to music.*

🔊 **C. Listen. Circle the word you hear.**

1. swimming   shopping   2. studying   saying

3. listening   looking   4. talking   teaching

5. using   eating   6. going   getting

💬 **D. Talk about things you like a lot and things you like a little.**

I like shopping.

Do you like it a lot or a little?

I like it a lot.

Oh, I like shopping a little.

Sounds of English

Contractions with *not*

🔊 Speakers use contractions to make negative statements about people and things. Listen to the full and contracted forms.

I			
You	do not → don't	know.	
We			
They			

I am not	→ I'm not	ready.
We are not	→ We're not	
They are not	→ They're not	
It is not	→ It's not	

Note: *I don't know* often sounds like *I dunno.*

🔊 **E. Listen and repeat.**

1. Are you a student here?   No, I'm not.
2. Is it easy?   No, it's not.
3. Do we have class now?   No, we don't.
4. Are they busy?   No, they're not.
5. Do you like shopping?   No, I don't.

🔊 **F. Listen to the speakers. Circle the word or words to make a sentence about the conversation.**

1. It's   *a good*   *not a good*   restaurant.
2. They   *like*   *don't like*   computer games.
3. You're   *busy*   *not busy*   today.
4. They   *like*   *don't like*   swimming.
5. We   *like*   *don't like*   the gym.

🔊 **G. Listen to the speakers and check (✓) the words you hear.**

A B

1. ☐ It's   ✓ It's not   easy to speak English.
2. ☐ I'm   ☐ I'm not   a new student.
3. ☐ We   ☐ We don't   like music.
4. ☐ I'm   ☐ I'm not   busy today.
5. ☐ It's   ☐ It's not   important to have a lot of friends.

Chant

GO ONLINE for the Chapter 2 Vocabulary & Grammar Chant

ACADEMIC LISTENING

A. Check (✓) the topics you like.

☐ movies   ☐ food   ☐ music

☐ sports   ☐ nature   ☐ technology

B. Stand up and walk around. Ask people about their interests. Say, "What kind of…?" Use the words in the box to help.

| beautiful | exciting | fun | interesting | new | popular | quiet |

> Do you like movies?

> Yes, I do.

> What kind of movies?

> I like exciting movies.

C. Listen to the first section. What does the speaker talk about? Check (✓) the correct answer.

☐ using technology

☐ student activities

☐ books for classes

D. Listen to the whole talk. Complete the questions you hear.

1. Do you like _____?

2. Do you like _____?

3. Do you like _____?

Listening for a speaker's questions

🔊 When speakers give talks, they sometimes use questions to organize their ideas. Listen to the examples.

Do you want to meet new people? Join a club, and...

Do you want to have fun? Get together with friends, and...

Do you want to see new places? Go for walks with...

GO ONLINE
for more practice

🔊 **E. Listen to the talk again. Circle the activities for each question.**

1. sports   *playing soccer*   *swimming*   *exercising at the gym*

2. movies   *talk about movies*   *see a movie on a phone*   *watch a movie downtown*

3. nature   *nature walks*   *the beach*   *beautiful parks*

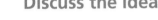

🔊 **F. Listen to the talk again. Then ask and answer the questions with a partner.**

Partner A	Partner B
1. What does Rick think about clubs? 3. What does the movie club do? 5. What does the nature club do?	2. What sports does Rick talk about? 4. Where does the movie club go? 6. Where does the nature club go?

Discuss the Ideas

G. Work with a partner. Practice asking and answering the questions.

Partner A	Partner B
Why is this class important? Why are friends good?	You practice speaking. You have fun. You can meet interesting teachers. They listen to you. You can play games.

▲▲▲ SPEAKING

Speaking Task Sharing interests with others

Step 1 PREPARE

Pronunciation Skill

Stress on nouns

 English speakers put stress on nouns when they speak. In words with two or more syllables, you usually stress one syllable. Listen and repeat.

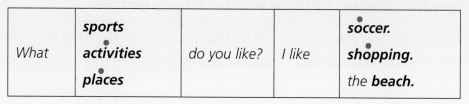

What	**sports**			**soccer.**
	activities	do you like?	I like	**shopping.**
	places			the **beach.**

 A. Listen and repeat.

A	B	A
1. What sports do you like?	Sports?	Yeah, sports.
2. Do you play soccer?	Soccer?	Yeah, soccer.
3. Do you like music?	Music?	Yeah, music.
4. Where do you go on campus?	On campus?	Yeah, on campus.
5. Where do you go for fun?	Fun?	Yeah, fun.
6. Do you watch movies?	Movies?	Yeah, movies.

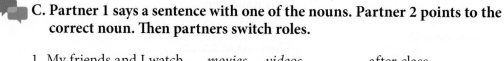 **B. Work with a partner. Ask and answer the questions in Activity A.**

C. Partner 1 says a sentence with one of the nouns. Partner 2 points to the correct noun. Then partners switch roles.

1. My friends and I watch	*movies*	*videos*	after class.
2. I like	*shopping*	*swimming*	for fun.
3. My family and I go to	*the beach*	*the park*	sometimes.
4. My classmates and I play	*games*	*soccer*	on the weekend.
5. We listen to	*music*	*concerts*	on campus.
6. We exercise at	*the gym*	*the park*	together.

D. Listen. Complete the conversation with the words from the box.

concert	friends	music	students	swimming	~~the beach~~

Kenji: Hey, Han. What do you do on the weekend?

Han: I usually go to _____the beach_____.

Kenji: Yeah, the beach is great. I really like _____.

Han: What do you do on the weekend?

Kenji: I like listening to _____. Sometimes I go downtown and see

a _____.

Han: Really? Do you go with _____?

Kenji: Uh, yeah, I usually go with the music club. We get together as a big group.

Han: Oh, are you in a music club?

Kenji: Yeah, it's for _____. Do you want to join?

Han: Maybe. What kind of music is it?

Kenji: Oh, all different kinds. Are you interested? You can come with me.

Han: Sure. I'll try it.

GO ONLINE
to practice the
conversation

 E. Work with a partner. Practice the conversation in Activity D.

 F. Work with a partner. Use the words in the charts and your own ideas to ask and answer questions.

Partner 1			Partner 2		
What kind of	beaches places music parks movies activities	do you like?	I like	quiet popular beautiful fun interesting exciting	beaches. places. music. parks. movies. activities.

A. Circle the words and phrases that you like.

Things		Activities	Places	
computers movies sports	good food nature technology	listening to music playing computer games shopping swimming walking watching movies	downtown movie theaters restaurants	home parks beach

Speaking Skill

Explaining activities with frequency adverbs

Speakers use the frequency expressions *usually, sometimes,* and *almost never* to say they do activities a lot or a little. Listen to the examples.

usually ⌐a lot
Where do you go?   *I **usually** go downtown.*

sometimes
What do you do after class?   ***Sometimes** I go for a walk.*

almost never ⌐a little
Do you like games?   *Not much. I **almost never** play.*

 B. Use the Word Partners box and frequency adverbs to talk about your activities and habits.

C. Use the words in the chart and your own ideas to complete the conversations.

I My classmates and I My friends and I We	often usually almost never	listen to music. meet in restaurants. play computer games. play sports.
Sometimes	I my friends and I we	go shopping. go to the beach. watch movies.

1. A: What do you do to learn English?

   B: _____

2. A: Where do you go on campus?

   B: _____

3. A: Where do you go downtown?

   B: _____

Speaking Task

Sharing interests with others

1. Write a list of your activities. Then read the questions and think about your answers.

> **Questions**
>
> When do you do it?
>
> Who do you do it with?
>
> Where do you do it?

Activity 1: _____ Activity 2: _____

Activity 3: _____

2. Close your book and form groups of three. Take turns telling about your activities.

3. Ask your partners questions about their activities.

Step 3 REPORT

Complete the sentences. Use the sentences and your notes to write a report.

1. _____ is similar to me. We like _____.

2. _____ is different from me. I like _____.

   He/she likes _____.

Step 4 REFLECT

Checklist

Check (✓) the things you learned in Chapter 2.

○ I learned language for talking about interests and activities.

○ I understood people talking about activities.

○ I talked to partners about their interests and activities.

Discussion Question

What activities are popular in your class? Why?

- Use *will* with *I, you,* and *we*
- Listen for *here* and *there*
- Recognize reductions of *want to, like to,* and *have to*
- Listen for sequence words
- Practice linking with the schwa /ə/ sound
- Make plans to get together with classmates

▲ **VOCABULARY** ▶ Oxford 2000 ✎ words to talk about places on campus

Learn Words

🔊 **A. Label each picture with the correct word. Then listen and repeat the words and phrases.**

buildings	coffee	entertainment	famous	museum	plans	~~tour~~	video

1.

_____*tour*_____ the campus

2.

academic _____

3.

a _____ shop

4.

musical _____

5.

make travel _____

6.

create a _____

7.

_____ people

8.

an art _____

Will with *I, you,* and *we*

🔊 Speakers use *will* before verbs to tell about the future. In spoken English, the sound is reduced to *I'll*, *you'll*, and *we'll*. Listen to the examples.

> **I will** show you the fitness center. → **I'll** show you the fitness center.
>
> **We will** tour the campus. → **We'll** tour the campus.
>
> **You will** see the academic buildings. → **You'll** see the academic buildings.

🔊 **B. Listen and check (✓) the word you hear.**

	A		B		C	
1.	☐ I'll	✓	You'll	☐	We'll	go downtown.
2.	☐ I'll	☐	You'll	☐	We'll	read about it.
3.	☐ I'll	☐	You'll	☐	We'll	make a plan.
4.	☐ I'll	☐	You'll	☐	We'll	watch a movie.
5.	☐ I'll	☐	You'll	☐	We'll	tour the city.
6.	☐ I'll	☐	You'll	☐	We'll	talk to her.

💬 **C. Work with a partner. Partner A says a sentence from Activity B. Partner B says the letter of the correct column. Then partners switch roles.**

🔊 **D. Listen to the statements. Circle *the future* if you hear a reduction with *will*. Circle *now* if you don't.**

1. now	(the future)		2. now	the future	
3. now	the future		4. now	the future	
5. now	the future		6. now	the future	

💬 **E. Work with a partner. Talk about a place to meet.**

Partner A		Partner B	
I'll meet you	in the library. at a coffee shop. after class.	OK, I'll	see you later. take my computer. be there soon.

Learn Phrases

🔊 **A. Match each phrase to the correct picture. Then listen and repeat.**

come here to drink coffee	show **world cultures**
exercise at **the fitness center**	**spend a lot of money** on food
learn about **the entertainment business**	**use equipment** to make things
look for information online	visit **a history museum**

1.

2.

3.

4.

5.

6.

7.

8.

B. **Listen to the speakers. Circle the word or phrase that completes the description of each one.**

1. The teacher wants students to learn about	*buildings.*	*music.*
2. The student wants to work in	*science.*	*the entertainment business.*
3. The partners are discussing	*popular videos.*	*famous museums.*
4. People spend a lot of money	*at restaurants.*	*shopping online.*
5. The teacher is showing	*pictures of famous art.*	*a popular video.*
6. The speaker is asking questions about	*sports equipment.*	*exercise classes.*

 C. **Read the questions and answers. Then practice with a partner. Partner A asks a question. Partner B answers. Then partners switch roles.**

Partner A	Partner B		
1. What do you do online?	watch funny videos	post pictures	read about famous people
2. Where do you go for entertainment?	sports centers	movie theaters	restaurants
3. What will you do to exercise?	go to a fitness center	go for walks	do sports
4. What do you do in museums?	study world cultures	see art	learn about history
5. How do you relax?	watch movies	visit friends	play computer games
6. What will you spend money on?	clothes	games	technology

How do you relax?   I watch movies.

D. **Work with a partner. Partner A completes the sentence with a word or phrase. Partner B guesses the topic. Then partners switch roles.**

Partner A		Partner B	
I come here to	eat lunch with friends. study for class. play soccer. spend money on clothes. see art and culture. exercise. watch a movie.	It's	the library. a store downtown. a theater. the fitness center. a museum. a park.

GO ONLINE
for more practice

Vocabulary **47**

▲▲ LISTENING

CONVERSATION

🔊 **A. Listen to the conversation. Where are the speakers? Circle the correct answer.**

on a walk in a nature park   *at a movie theater downtown*   *on a college campus*

🔊 **B. Listen to the conversation again. Number the places in the order the speakers see them.**

_____ the fitness center   _____ the academic buildings   _____ the student center

Listening Strategy

Listening for *here* and *there*

🔊 Speakers use expressions with *here* and *there* to talk about distance. *Here* often partners with *this* to show that something is near or close. *There* shows that something is far or not close.

Sometimes people use *here* and *there* as pronouns. Listen to the examples.

here = the student center

This is the student center. A lot of clubs meet here.

here = coffee shop

I like this coffee shop. I'm here a lot.

there = computer room

How about the computer room? We can work there.

GO ONLINE
for more practice

🔊 **C. Listen to the conversation again. Complete the sentences about things you can find in each place.**

a coffee shop	sports fields	~~a lot of clubs~~	the business school
exercise equipment	the science building	history classes	

The student center	The academic buildings	The fitness center
___A lot of clubs___ meet here.	_____ is over there.	There is _____ here in the gym.
There is _____, too.	And here is _____.	Do you see the _____ over there?

48   Unit 1 | Chapter 3

Reductions of *want to*, *like to*, and *have to*

When speakers say *want to*, *have to*, or *like to* + verb, it sometimes sounds like *wanna*, *hafta*, or *liketa*. Listen to the examples.

Do you want to go? →	*Duya* **wanna** *go?*	*I* **wanna** *go.*	*I don't* **wanna** *go.*
Do you have to study? →	*Duya* **hafta** *study?*	*I* **hafta** *study.*	*I don't* **hafta** *study.*
Do you like to read? →	*Duya* **liketa** *read?*	*I* **liketa** *read.*	*I don't* **liketa** *read.*

D. Listen and repeat each question and answer.

1. Do you want to meet here?   No, I want to meet there.

2. Do you like to study nature?   No, I like to shop in stores.

3. Do you want to see a movie?   No, I have to meet a friend.

4. Do you want to look online?   No, I have to go to class.

5. Do you have to go to work?   No, I have to go downtown.

6. Do you want to come with me?   No, I have to stay home.

E. Listen to the speakers. Check (✓) the statement you hear.

A   B

1. [✓] I want to go downtown.   [ ] I want a place downtown.

2. [ ] I have to meet my friends.   [ ] I have many friends.

3. [ ] I like to watch movies.   [ ] I always go to movies.

4. [ ] I want to exercise with you.   [ ] I want more equipment, too.

5. [ ] We like to see museums.   [ ] We like coffee with friends.

6. [ ] We have to go now.   [ ] We have a class now.

Chant

GO ONLINE
for the
Chapter 3
Vocabulary &
Grammar Chant

F. Practice asking and answering the questions in Activity D with a partner.

A. Match each topic to the correct picture.

1. art and entertainment   2. science and technology   3. history and culture

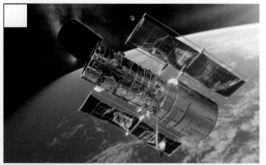

🔊 **B. Listen to the first section. Circle the correct answer.**

1. Who is speaking?	*a teacher*	*a singer*
2. Who is the class for?	*new students*	*English students*
3. What is the class?	*College Skills 101*	*The Business of Entertainment*

🔊 **C. Listen to the whole talk. Number the parts in the correct order.**

_____ history and culture   _____ art and entertainment   _____ science and technology

Listening Strategy

Listening for for sequence words

🔊 Speakers use *first, second, third,* and sometimes *finally* to show time order. Listen to the examples.

> *It takes time to learn new vocabulary.*
>
> **First,** *we learn new words.*
>
> **Second,** *we do an activity in our books.*
>
> **Third,** *we practice with a partner.*

GO ONLINE
for more
practice

D. Listen to the talk again. Draw a line where each part ends, and write *first part*, *second part*, and *third part* to organize the notes.

first part	listen to music
_____	watch videos
_____	create a video
_____	go to parks
_____	use equipment
_____	discuss history and culture
_____	read books
_____	visit museums

E. Listen to the talk again. Then ask and answer the questions with a partner.

Partner A	Partner B
1. Who is the class for?	2. Why are students taking the class?
3. What will they do first?	4. What will they do second?
5. What will they do third?	6. How will they work as a team?

Discuss the Ideas

F. Choose three activities that you like to do on the weekend. Write *first*, *second*, and *third* to show sequence.

_____ go downtown to see a movie

_____ make and post videos online

_____ go for a walk in nature

_____ meet friends at a coffee shop

_____ exercise at the fitness center

_____ visit history and art museums

G. Share your sequence of activities with a partner. Are you similar or different?

Speaking Task

Making plans to get together with classmates

Step 1 PREPARE

Pronunciation Skill

Linking with the schwa /ə/ sound

🔊 The schwa sound, /ə/, appears in *a*, *an*, *the*, *to*, *about*, and many other words we use with adjectives and nouns, but it is sometimes hard to hear. Listen to the examples.

> *It's a good idea.* → *its a good idea*
>
> *spend a lot of money* → *spend a lot a money*
>
> *get a coffee* → *get a coffee*
>
> *ask about the time* → *ask about the time*

Note: *A* or *an* is used to introduce one thing. *The* is used before one or more specific things that we know.

GO ONLINE
for more
practice

🔊 **A. Listen and repeat the words, phrases, and sentences.**

1. a movie   a movie about a man   It's a movie about a man and a computer.
2. a game   a game at the student center   There's a game at the student center.
3. a coffee   a cup of coffee   How about a cup of coffee?
4. a park   at a park   Do you want to meet at a park?
5. a concert see a concert   Let's see a concert.

🔊 **B. Listen and check (✓) the sentence you hear.**

	A		B
1.	✓ I want to go, too.	☐	I want good food.
2.	☐ We'll meet a new friend.	☐	We'll meet new friends.
3.	☐ That's a good idea.	☐	That's good for eating.
4.	☐ I need to go online.	☐	I'm never here on time.
5.	☐ That's a good plan.	☐	There's my new plan.

GO ONLINE
to practice the
conversation

 C. Practice with a partner. Partner A says a sentence from Activity B. Partner B
says the letter of the correct column. Then partners switch roles.

 D. Listen and complete the conversation with the words in the box. Use some
words more than once.

a	about	of	the	to

Van: We don't have _____ to _____ study tonight. Let's go out.

Grimilda: That's _____ good idea. Where do you want

_____ go?

Van: How about _____ restaurant?

Grimilda: Hmm. I don't want to spend a lot _____ money.

Van: OK, _____ coffee shop?

Grimilda: I'd like to get some exercise first. Do you like _____ fitness

center downtown?

Van: Really? Exercise? I'll go with you, but I won't work out. I'll just watch!

Grimilda: That won't be fun for you! Let's do something together.

Van: Do you want to see _____ movie?

Grimilda: Sure. There's a funny one _____ college students.

Van: OK, I'll look online and check _____ movie times.

 E. Work with a partner. Practice the conversation in Activity D.

 F. Use the words in the chart and your own ideas to practice talking about
things you like and don't like. Partner A says a sentence, and Partner B
responds with a suggestion. Then partners switch roles.

Partner A		Partner B	
I want	to get some exercise. to go downtown. to have fun.	OK, do you want to go to	a gym? a concert? a soccer game?
		Umm, I don't want to spend a lot of money. Let's	go for a walk. stay at home. watch a movie go online.

I want to get some exercise.

Umm, I don't want to spend a lot of money. Let's go for a walk.

Step 2 SPEAK

A. Check (✓) the activities you want to do with friends.

☐ play sports   ☐ make a video   ☐ go to a museum

☐ go for a walk in nature   ☐ see a movie   ☐ go shopping

☐ play games at the student center   ☐ try a new restaurant

Word Partners

meet downtown

meet here

meet there

meet after class

meet at a restaurant

GO ONLINE
to practice
word partners

Speaking Skill

Making suggestions

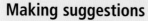 To make a plan with a group, speakers need to respond to suggestions by saying *yes* or *no* politely. Listen to the examples.

Suggestion	Yes	No
Let's go to a museum.	Sure, let's meet after class.	Sorry, I don't have time.
Do you want to meet here?	OK, sounds good.	Umm, let's meet at a coffee shop.

 B. Use the chart in the Speaking Skill box and your own ideas to practice deciding on a place to meet with a partner.

Do you want to see a movie?

Sure, let's meet downtown.

 C. Practice making plans. Partner A makes a suggestion. Partner B says *yes* or *no* or makes a new suggestion. Then partners switch roles.

Partner A	Partner B
Do you want to see a movie? Let's exercise at the fitness center after class. Do you want to play a computer game later? Do you want to go shopping with me? How about a visit to a museum?	Yes... No...

Speaking Task

Making plans to get together with classmates

1. Form a group of three. Take turns making suggestions for a fun day. Then write your plan in the chart.

	Activity	When	Where to meet
First			
Second			
Third			

2. Form a group of three new partners. Take turns presenting your plan. Listen to your partners' plans and make suggestions.

3. Work together. Choose a plan that everybody likes.

Step 3 REPORT

Fill in the report with your plan or write it on paper.

My friends and I have a plan. First, we want to _____. We will

meet _____. Second, we _____. Third,

we _____. Finally, we will meet _____.

Step 4 REFLECT

Checklist

Check (✓) the things you learned in Chapter 3.

○ I learned language for talking about future plans.

○ I understood people talking about college classes and activities.

○ I made plans with partners and wrote a report.

Discussion Question

Do you like to make plans with a big noisy group or a small quiet group?

Look at the word bank for Unit 1. Check (✓) the words you know. Circle the words you want to learn better.

OXFORD 2000 🔑

Adjectives	Nouns			Verbs	
busy	art	hand	restaurant	come	relax
confused	beach	history	room	create	shop
exciting	building	lunch	team	drink	show
famous	business	money	technology	exercise	spend
friendly	center	movie	theater	find	swim
fun	clothes	museum	thing	get	use
helpful	club	music	time	join	visit
interesting	coffee	nature	video	know	watch
nervous	culture	night	walk	look	work
noisy	entertainment	place	weekend	make	worry
popular	equipment	plan	world	raise	
quiet					
ready					
special					

PRACTICE WITH THE OXFORD 2000 🔑

A. Use the chart. Match adjectives with nouns.

1. _____a famous theater_____   2. _____

3. _____   4. _____

5. _____   6. _____

B. Use the chart. Match verbs with nouns.

1. _____spend money_____   2. _____

3. _____   4. _____

5. _____   6. _____

C. Use the chart. Match verbs with adjective noun partners.

1. _find interesting restaurants_   2. _____

3. _____   4. _____

5. _____   6. _____

UNIT **2** Places

CHAPTER **4** ## What's Your New Place Like?

▲ **VOCABULARY**
- Oxford 2000 🔑 words to talk about living preferences

▲▲ **LISTENING**
- Listening for hesitations
- Listening for reasons

▲▲▲ **SPEAKING**
- Practicing intonation of choice questions
- Surveying others about their living preferences

CHAPTER **5** ## What Can You Do There?

▲ **VOCABULARY**
- Oxford 2000 🔑 words to talk about outdoor activities

▲▲ **LISTENING**
- Listening for time
- Listening for place

▲▲▲ **SPEAKING**
- Practicing reductions of *can* in *wh-* questions
- Describing a place tourists can visit

CHAPTER **6** ## Where Are You Going?

▲ **VOCABULARY**
- Oxford 2000 🔑 words to talk about getting around the city

▲▲ **LISTENING**
- Listening for interjections
- Listening for effects with *so*

▲▲▲ **SPEAKING**
- Practicing linking with plural *-s*
- Giving directions to a local place

UNIT WRAP UP ## Extend Your Skills

What's Your New Place Like?

- Use *more/less* + adjectives
- Listen for hesitations
- Recognize stress on *-er/-ier* adjectives
- Listen for reasons
- Practice intonation of choice questions
- Survey others about their living preferences

▲ VOCABULARY ▶ Oxford 2000 ♪ words to talk about living preferences

Learn Words

🔊 **A. Label each picture with the correct word. Then listen and repeat the words and phrases.**

| bright | colorful | comfortable | dark | pretty | ~~simple~~ | strange | tall |

1.

a _____simple_____ phone

2.

_____ furniture

3.

_____ houses

4.

a _____ light

5.

a _____ city

6.

_____ windows

7.

a _____ building

8.

a _____ street

More/less with adjectives

🔊 Comparative adjectives show differences between two nouns. Use *more* and *less* before longer adjectives. Listen to the examples.

*The city is **more colorful** at night.*

*They sell **less expensive** furniture.*

🔊 Link *more* and *less* with adjectives that start with a vowel sound. When you link, there is no pause. Listen to the examples.

more‿important   *less‿important*

🔊 **B. Listen to each phrase. Check (✓) if the phrase is linked.**

1. ☐ more exciting

2. ☐ more comfortable

3. ☐ more expensive

4. ☐ less noisy

5. ☐ less unhappy

6. ☐ less interested

 C. Work with a partner. Use the phrases to compare the two places.

more/less beautiful	more/less colorful	more/less fun for young people	more/less interesting	more/less expensive

Place A

Place B

Example: Place A is more beautiful.

Learn Phrases

🔊 **A. Match each phrase to the correct picture. Then listen and repeat.**

a crowded area downtown	**cost** a lot of **money**
drive close to the cars	has **a simple bedroom**
put pictures **on the wall**	**save money for** the future
take the bus downtown	tall **apartment buildings**

1.

2.

3.

4.

5.

6.

7.

8.

B. Listen to each conversation. Circle the phrase that completes the description of it.

1. Her bedroom has   *colorful windows.*   *colorful walls.*

2. The apartment has   *comfortable furniture.*   *dark furniture.*

3. She has   *a simple home.*   *a strange home.*

4. He lives in   *a crowded area.*   *a quiet area.*

5. They need to   *take the bus.*   *take a car.*

C. Circle two words that pair with the first word.

1. crowded   *bus*   *light*   *street*

2. save   *food*   *time*   *downtown*

3. simple   *city*   *apartment*   *furniture*

4. colorful   *walls*   *close*   *buildings*

5. dark   *light*   *area*   *bedroom*

6. take my   *car*   *house*   *phone*

 D. Work with a partner. Ask and answer the questions.

Partner A	Partner B
1. Do you have an apartment? 3. Do you live close to shops? 5. Do you take the bus to school? 7. Do you have a colorful bedroom?	2. Do you have a house? 4. Do you live close to the city? 6. Do you drive home? 8. Do you have pictures on your walls?

E. Close your book. Work with one or two partners. Ask and answer questions about your neighborhood.

Is your neighborhood pretty?

Does it have a lot of shops?

Do you like it?

GO ONLINE for more practice

▲▲ LISTENING

CONVERSATION

🔊 **A. Listen to the conversation. Circle where Hilary wants to live.**

outside the city   *close to town*   downtown

🔊 **B. Listen to the conversation again. Circle the correct answer.**

1. Hilary needs   *two* *three*   bedrooms.

2. She prefers   *newer* *older* apartments.

3. She wants a place with   *lighter* *darker* rooms.

Listening Strategy

Listening for hesitations

🔊 Speakers use hesitation words like *well*, *so*, and *umm* to say that they need time to think. After hesitation words, speakers usually take a pause. Listen to the examples.

> A: **So**...are you my new neighbor?
>
> B: **Umm**...I think so. I'm in Apartment 11.
>
> A: **Well**...then we are neighbors! I'm in Apartment 12.

GO ONLINE
for more
practice

🔊 **C. Listen to the parts of the conversation again. Check (✓) the hesitation expression you hear.**

1. ☑ well... ☐ so...   2. ☐ so... ☐ umm...

3. ☐ so... ☐ well...   4. ☐ well... ☐ umm...

 D. Practice the conversations with a partner. Then switch roles.

1. A: So...are you in college?
   B: Well...no. But I will be next year.

2. A: Is Jackson Street close to here?
   B: Umm...I'm not sure.

3. A: This apartment is really small!
   B: Well....at least it's downtown, right?

4. A: So...do you want to go eat?
   B: Well...I'm not really hungry now.

5. A: Why is this area so popular?
   B: Well...it has the best restaurants.

6. A: When do you want to meet?
   B: Umm...How about 7?

Stress on *-er/-ier* adjectives

For one-syllable adjectives, *-er* is added to an adjective to show comparison. Comparative adjectives with *-er* have two syllables. The stress is on the first syllable. Listen to the examples.

small → sm**all**er   cheap → **cheap**er

For two-syllable adjectives that end in *-y*, *-ier* is used to show comparison. Comparative adjectives with *-ier* have three syllables. The stress is on the first syllable. Listen to the examples.

pretty → pr**ett**ier   noisy → n**ois**ier

Some comparative adjectives change to new words. Listen to the examples.

good → better   bad → worse

E. Listen to each word and phrase. Check (✓) the phrase you hear.

A

1. ☐ a cheap apartment
2. ☐ a nice café
3. ☐ bright bedrooms
4. ☐ a pretty street
5. ☐ a quiet place

B

1. ✓ a cheaper apartment
2. ☐ a nicer café
3. ☐ brighter bedrooms
4. ☐ a prettier street
5. ☐ a quieter place

F. Work with a partner. Use the comparative adjectives in the box to compare the two pictures.

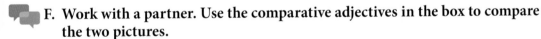

better   brighter   darker   noisier   older   prettier   quieter   smaller

Street A

Street B

Chant

GO ONLINE
for the
Chapter 4
Vocabulary &
Grammar Chant

ACADEMIC LISTENING

A. Check (✓) the things you prefer in a home. Share your ideas with a partner.

1. ☐ being in a quiet area   ☐ being in a fun area

2. ☐ living in the city   ☐ living outside the city

3. ☐ being closer to shops   ☐ being closer to nature

B. Listen to the first section of the interview. Circle the correct answer.

1. The interview is about   *a new book.*   *a new movie.*

2. Micro apartments are   *very small.*   *very big.*

3. Micro apartments have furniture   *in the rooms.*   *in the walls.*

C. Listen to the second section of the interview. Complete the statements with *more* or *less* to make them true.

1. People spend _____ money on micro apartments.

2. Living downtown is _____ fun.

3. People have _____ things to do downtown.

4. There are _____ restaurants.

5. There are _____ places to shop.

Listening Strategy

Listening for reasons

Speakers give reasons to explain their ideas. Reasons answer the question *Why?* To introduce a reason, speakers often say *because.* Listen to the example.

> A: Why do people want micro apartments?
>
>   reason
> B: Well, **because** they're cheaper.

Speakers can use other phrases to explain a reason.

> ***It's also because*** they're cheaper.
>
> ***Another reason*** is that they're cheaper.

GO ONLINE
for more
practice

🔊 **D. Listen and match the phrase to the correct statement.**

Another reason is that	It's fun because	It's also because

1. _____ micro apartments are downtown.

2. _____ people live closer to everything.

3. _____ downtown is popular.

🔊 **E. Listen to the interview again. Ask and answer the questions with a partner.**

Partner A	Partner B
1. What is a micro apartment?	2. Where do people find micro apartments?
3. Why do people want to live downtown?	4. Why do people like to walk to places?
5. Why do people want micro apartments?	6. What is another reason?

Discuss the Ideas

F. Read the statements. Circle your opinion.

1. It's better to live   *in a smaller apartment*   *in a bigger apartment.*

2. It's better to live   *in the center of the city.*   *outside the city.*

3. Micro apartments   *are good for my city.*   *are not good for my city.*

4. Micro apartments are better for *younger people*   *older people.*

G. Work with a partner. Partner A shares an opinion from Activity F. Partner B asks *Why?* Partner A give a reason with *because*. Then partners switch roles.

It's better to live in a bigger apartment.

Why?

Because you have more space.

▲▲▲ SPEAKING

Speaking Task

Surveying others about their living preferences

Step 1 PREPARE

Pronunciation Skill

Intonation of choice questions

🔊 Speakers use *Do you like...?* and *Do you prefer...?* to ask about what people like.

Do you like *history?*   **Do you prefer** *bigger cities?*

🔊 Speakers use *or* to give people a choice. When you ask choice questions, use rising and falling intonation. Listen to the examples.

A: *Do you like history* **or** *art?*   A: *Do you prefer bigger* **or** *smaller cities?*

B: *I like history.*   B: *I prefer smaller cities.*

GO ONLINE
for more
practice

🔊 **A. Listen and repeat.**

A	B
1. Do you like soccer?	Do you like soccer or football?
2. Do you like books?	Do you like books or movies?
3. Do you like computers?	Do you like computers or art?
4. Do you prefer coffee?	Do you prefer coffee or tea?
5. Do you prefer old furniture?	Do you prefer old or new furniture?
6. Do you prefer driving to places?	Do you prefer driving or walking to places?

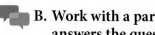 **B. Work with a partner. Partner A asks a question from Activity A. Partner B answers the question. Then partners switch roles.**

🔊 **C. Listen to the questions. Check (✓) the best answer.**

Yes/no answers	Choice answers
1. ☑ Yes, I do.	☐ I prefer apartments.
2. ☐ No, I don't.	☐ I prefer brighter bedrooms.
3. ☐ Yes, I do.	☐ I like spending money.
4. ☐ Yes, I do.	☐ I prefer quiet streets.
5. ☐ No, I don't.	☐ I like bigger apartments.

D. Work with a partner. Ask and answer the questions with *Do you like...?* or *Do you prefer...?*

Partner A	Partner B
1. ...noisy streets or quiet streets?	2. ...brighter rooms or darker rooms?
3. ...colorful homes or simple homes?	4. ...bigger cities or smaller cities?
5. ...living close to family or to friends?	6. ...being downtown or being in nature?
7. ...friendly or quiet neighbors?	8. ...small stores or big stores?
9. ...taking the bus or driving?	10. ...walking or biking to places?

E. Listen. Complete the conversation with the words from the box.

a little more	drive to school	in class	later	~~near work~~

A: So, do you want an apartment near school or _____ near work _____?

B: Umm...that's hard to say.

A: Well, do you spend more time _____ or at work?

B: I spend more time in class. I take four classes.

A: OK. So, apartments near your school are more expensive.

B: So, they cost a lot more or _____?

A: Only a little more, really.

B: That's OK, I guess.

A: OK, and do you bike or _____?

B: Umm...I like to bike. Why?

A: Well, it's a perfect area for bikers. There are lots of places to bike.

B: That sounds great!

A: OK. Let's look at some apartments near school then. Do you want to look now or _____?

B: Let's look now. I have class later.

A: Oh, right. OK, then.

 F. Work with a partner. Practice the conversation in Activity E.

GO ONLINE
to practice the conversation

Step 2 SPEAK

A. Think about the place you want to live. Check (✓) the things you prefer.

☐ living in the city   ☐ living outside the city

☐ older buildings   ☐ newer buildings

☐ a smaller apartment   ☐ a bigger apartment

Speaking Skill

Using *because* to add information

🔊 Speakers use *because* to give more information. *Because* often explains why people like or prefer something. Listen to the examples.

> I like cities **because** they're fun.
>
> I prefer an apartment **because** it's cheaper.

🔊 Speakers often reduce *because* to *'cuz*. It sounds shorter and softer. Listen to the examples.

> I like cities **'cuz** they're fun.
>
> I prefer an apartment **'cuz** it's cheaper.

B. Work with a partner. Use the words in the chart and your own ideas to describe what you like or prefer.

I like I prefer	a bigger place being close to shops having an apartment living in the city older buildings quieter areas a simpler home	because... 'cuz...

Word Partners

prefer living

prefer going

prefer doing

prefer having

prefer being

GO ONLINE
to practice
word partners

> I like a bigger place 'cuz I have a lot of furniture.

Speaking Task

Surveying classmates about their living preferences

1. Write two more questions in the chart. Then complete the survey about you.

	Me	Partner 1	Partner 2
Do you prefer an apartment or a house?			
_____			
_____			

2. Close your book. Work with two partners to ask and answer the survey questions.

Step 3 REPORT

Complete the sentences with information from your survey to write a report. Share your findings with the class to learn about popular places to live.

_____ prefers _____.

wants to be close to _____.

does not like _____.

_____ prefers _____.

wants to be close to _____.

does not like _____.

Step 4 REFLECT

Checklist

Check (✓) the things you learned in Chapter 4.

○ I learned language to describe living preferences.

○ I understood an interview about micro apartments.

○ I surveyed and reported on my classmates' living preferences.

Discussion Question

Are micro apartments better for young people?

CHAPTER 5 What Can You Do There?

- Use *can* for ability
- Listen for time
- Recognize *can* and *can't*
- Listen for place
- Practice reductions of *can* in *wh-* questions
- Describe a place tourists can visit

▲ VOCABULARY ▸ Oxford 2000 ✎ words to talk about outdoor activities

Learn Words

🔊 **A. Label each picture with the correct word. Then listen and repeat the words and phrases.**

| animals | desert | flowers | forest | hotel | mountains | path | ~~rocks~~ |

1.

strange _____rocks_____

2.

wild _____

3.

an expensive _____

4.

a walking _____

5.

a green _____

6.

colorful _____

7.

high in the _____

8.

a tour of the _____

Grammar Note

Can for ability

Speakers use *can* to talk about ability. *Can* is followed by verbs. Listen to the examples.

> You **can** <u>see</u> old buildings in my neighborhood.
>
> We **can** <u>play</u> soccer this afternoon. It's a nice day.

To ask a *yes/no* question, say *can* before the subject. Raise your voice at the end of the question. Listen to the examples.

> **Can** you see me?
>
> **Can** we take pictures?

B. Complete each statement with a phrase from the box. Then listen and check your answers.

~~can go~~	can have	can meet	can play	can see	can take

1. I want to go to the beach tomorrow. Maybe we _____ *can go* _____ together.

2. Your brother _____ soccer really well. Does he practice every day?

3. I _____ you later outside the cafeteria. OK?

4. You _____ many tall buildings in Houston. How about your city?

5. Let's go to the student center. We _____ fun there.

6. We _____ the bus and save some time.

C. Listen to each question and circle the answer you hear.

Question	*Yes* answer	*No* answer
1. Can you drive a car?	*Yes, I can.*	*No, I can't.*
2. Can you play basketball?	*Yes, I can.*	*No, I can't.*
3. Can you study after school?	*Yes, I can.*	*No, I can't.*
4. Can you drink a lot of coffee?	*Yes, I can.*	*No, I can't.*
5. Can you relax on the weekends?	*Yes, I can.*	*No, I can't.*
6. Can you post videos online?	*Yes, I can.*	*No, I can't.*

D. Work with a partner. Partner A asks a question from Activity C. Partner B answers with a *yes* or *no* answer. Then partners switch roles.

Learn Phrases

different **kinds of** flowers	**far away from** the city
go hiking with friends	**grow plants** in the garden
proud of her flower shop	**see details** in the flower
see a wild animal **up close**	**take pictures of** the beach

1.

2.

3.

4.

5.

6.

7.

8.

B. Listen to each conversation. Circle the correct answer.

1. How does she feel?	*proud*	*nervous*
2. What do they want to do?	*go biking*	*go hiking*
3. What kinds of flowers do they see?	*colorful flowers*	*strange flowers*
4. Where are the mountains?	*up close*	*far away*
5. Where do the flowers grow?	*in a garden*	*in the forest*

C. Think about your city. Complete the chart to describe where you can do the activities. Use the words from the box or your own ideas.

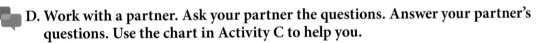

go hiking	go on a tour of the desert
go swimming	go to the beach
ride on bike paths	see mountains
take nature walks	visit museums

Downtown	Outside the city

D. Work with a partner. Ask your partner the questions. Answer your partner's questions. Use the chart in Activity C to help you.

1. What can you do downtown?

   What else can you do?

2. What can you do outside the city?

   What else can you do?

> What can you do downtown?

> You can ride on bike paths.

GO ONLINE
for more
practice

▲▲ LISTENING

CONVERSATION

🔊 **A. Listen to the conversation. Circle the correct answers.**

1. Where do they want to go?   *to the beach*   *to the desert*   *to the mountains*

2. What do they want to do?   *go swimming*   *go hiking*   *go downtown*

3. When will they leave?   *in the morning*   *in the afternoon*   *in the evening*

Listening Strategy

Listening for time

🔊 Time signals explain when something happens. Speakers often use *today* to signal the present and *tomorrow* to signal the future. Listen to the examples.

> It's cold **today**, but it will be nicer **tomorrow**.

To show the time of day, speakers use signals like *in the morning, in the afternoon,* and *in the evening*. Listen to the examples.

> He runs **in the morning**.   We relax **in the afternoon**.

GO ONLINE
for more
practice

🔊 **B. Listen to the conversation again. Write the time signals you hear.**

Tony: Derek, hi.

Derek: Oh, hey, Tony. What's up?

Tony: Sorry, I know you're busy _____today_____. But I have an idea for

_____.

Derek: Oh, yeah? What's that?

Tony: Well, some friends and I want to go hiking in the mountains. Can you come?

Derek: The mountains? Sure, I can! What time _____?

Tony: We can go in the morning or _____.

Derek: I can't go _____. I have to work early.

Tony: OK. Then we can leave _____.

Derek: Yes, that'll work.

Tony: Great. I'll call my friends, and we'll make a plan. Then I'll call you back.

Derek: OK, sounds good. Talk to you later _____ then.

Tony: Sounds good. Thanks! Bye!

💬 **C. Practice the conversation in Activity B with a partner. Use different time signals.**

Recognizing *can* and *can't*

🔊 When speakers say *can*, it is often reduced, so it sounds fast. Listen to the examples.

> *I* **can** *go with you.* → *I* **kn** *go with you.*

> *You* **can** *see lots of animals there.* → *You* **kn** *see lots of animals there.*

🔊 When speakers say *can't*, it is stressed, so it sounds louder. The final /t/ is not spoken. Listen to the examples.

> *Sorry, I* **can't** *get together today.* → *Sorry, I* **KAN'** *get together today.*

> *We* **can't** *visit the museum tomorrow.* → *We* **KAN'** *visit the museum tomorrow.*

🔊 **D. Listen to each statement. Check (✓) the phrase you hear.**

A	B
1. ☐ I can meet…	✓ I can't meet…
2. ☐ You can use…	☐ You can't use…
3. ☐ I can see…	☐ I can't see….
4. ☐ We can leave…	☐ We can't leave…
5. ☐ You can come…	☐ You can't come…
6. ☐ I can hear…	☐ I can't hear…

🔊 **E. Complete each statement with *can* or *can't*. Then listen and check your answers.**

1. A: You _____ walk to school today. It's raining hard.

   B: OK. Can I take your car then?

2. A: I _____ meet you in the afternoon.

   B: OK. Let's meet outside.

3. A: We _____ go swimming today. How about tomorrow?

   B: Tomorrow's good.

4. A: I _____ see. It's too dark.

   B: Oh, sorry. I'll turn on the lights.

F. Practice the conversations in Activity E with a partner.

Chant

GO ONLINE
for the
Chapter 5
Vocabulary &
Grammar Chant

A. Check (✓) the things you can see in a forest. Share your ideas with a partner.

☐ animals ☐ cars ☐ rocks

☐ buildings ☐ plants ☐ trees

B. Listen to the first section. Check (✓) the picture that matches the topic.

C. Listen to the whole talk. Then read each question and circle the correct answer.

1. Do the tourists walk slowly or quickly?

   The tourists walk *slowly* *quickly.*

2. Do the women want to see wild animals or plants?

   The women want to see *wild animals* *plants.*

3. Do the women see the moss up close or far away?

   They see the moss *up close* *far away.*

4. Do buildings in Japan have mossy gardens or mossy forests?

   They have mossy *gardens* *forests.*

5. Does moss grow well in the mountains or on the beach?

   It grows well *in the mountains* *on the beach.*

 D. Work with a partner. Ask and answer the questions in Activity C.

Listening Strategy

Listening for place

Speakers use the prepositions *at*, *in*, and *on* to tell about where something is. Listen to the examples.

> **In** <u>the mountains of Japan</u>, *tourists walk together slowly.*

> *People look* **at** <u>the moss</u> *up close, and they can see beautiful details.*

GO ONLINE
for more
practice

E. Listen to each statement. Complete each sentence with the phrase you hear.

at special hotels	in Japan	in Japan's forests	in nature	on the rocks

1. There are 1,800 kinds of moss _____.

2. Moss grows well _____ and the trees.

3. The Japanese like details _____.

4. Today, moss tours _____ are popular.

5. Tourists can stay _____ for moss tours.

F. Listen to the talk again. Ask and answer the questions with a partner.

Partner A	Partner B
1. What is moss?	2. Where do Japanese tourists see moss?
3. Where does moss grow well?	4. Why do the Japanese like moss?
5. What can people do on a moss tour?	6. What are the Japanese women proud of?

Discuss the Ideas

G. Think about your city. Check (✓) the things it has.

☐ beautiful forests   ☐ colorful flowers

☐ green mountains   ☐ historical places

☐ interesting museums   ☐ nice parks

☐ pretty gardens   ☐ wild animals

H. Work with a partner. Describe a city you like.

Partner A	Partner B
There are beautiful...	Wow! I'd like to see that.
You can see historical...	That sounds amazing!
People like...	Really, are there any...?
...grows there/here.	I want to learn more about...

Speaking Task Describing a place tourists can visit

Step 1 PREPARE

Pronunciation Skill

Reduction of *can* in *wh-* questions

🔊 When speakers ask a *yes/no* question with *can*, it is often stressed. Listen to the examples.

> **Can** you help me? → *KAN you help me?*
>
> **Can** we see it up close? → *KAN we see it up close?*

🔊 When speakers ask a *wh-* question, *can* is often reduced. Listen to the examples.

> What **can** you see? → *What kn you see?*
>
> When **can** we go? → *When kn we go?*

GO ONLINE
for more
practice

🔊 **A. Listen and repeat.**

A	**B**
1. Can we leave?	When can we leave?
2. Can you see?	What can you see?
3. Can I take it?	When can I take it?
4. Can they walk?	Where can they walk?
5. Can we help?	How can we help?
6. Can I go?	Who can I go with?

 B. Work with a partner. Partner A says a question from Activity A. Partner B points to the correct question. Then partners switch roles.

🔊 **C. Listen to the questions. Write *Can you* or *Do you*.**

1. _____*Do you*_____ like your city?

2. _____ ride a bike?

3. _____ speak English?

4. _____ exercise often?

5. _____ hear me well?

6. _____ like to go hiking?

D. Ask and answer the questions in Activity C with a partner.

> Do you like your city?

> Yes, I do. It's a fun place to live.

E. Listen. Use the phrases from the box to complete the conversation.

Can I get	Can I meet	Can you call	~~Can you come~~	Can you leave

A: So, Eliza. _____Can you come_____ on Thursday?

B: Come to what?

A: To the art club meeting.

B: Oh yeah! That's right. _____ there late?

A: I'm not sure. Why?

B: Well…I have class until 3:15.

A: Oh, I see. _____ earlier?

B: Maybe. I can ask my teacher. Why?

A: Well, we're all going to the art museum together. But we leave at 3.

B: Hmm… _____ you there? I can go right after class.

A: Sure, that'll be fine.

B: OK. And how can I find you guys?

A: _____ me when you get there?

B: Yes, I think I have your number on my phone.

GO ONLINE
to practice the
conversation

F. Work with a partner. Practice the conversation in Activity E.

G. Form groups of three. Partner A thinks of a place. Partners B and C ask *wh-* questions and try to guess the place. Then partners switch roles.

a beach	a fitness center	a museum	a restaurant	the mountains
a big city	a library	a park	downtown	

> What do you see there?

> You usually see people and water.

> What can you do there?

> You can swim.

Step 2 SPEAK

A. Write the names of popular places in your city. Then write notes about each place.

Place	What can you see there?	What can you do there?

Speaking Skill

Describing a place

🔊 When people describe a place, they usually give details about what it looks like and what you can do there. Speakers often use *there is* and *there are* to give descriptive details about places. Listen to the examples.

> *The park is in the mountains.* **There are** *tall trees, and* **there's** *a beautiful walking path.*

🔊 Speakers use *you can* to tell people what they can do at a place. Listen to the examples.

> **You can** *walk on the trails with friends, or* **you can** *take a tour.*

 B. Work with a partner. Use the words in the charts and your own ideas to describe your place.

There's	a	beautiful colorful historic important	desert. forest. park. river.
There are	a lot of	interesting pretty small strange	animals. buildings. flowers. trees.

You can	have fun going to... learn about... take pictures of... take a tour of... see a lot of...

> I like Mason Square. It's downtown. There's a lot of history. You can see a lot of old buildings.

Word Partners

a lot of buildings

a lot of history

a lot of people

a lot of time

a lot of tourists

GO ONLINE
to practice
word partners

Speaking Task

Describing a place tourists can visit

1. Look at your notes in Activity A. Organize your ideas in the chart.

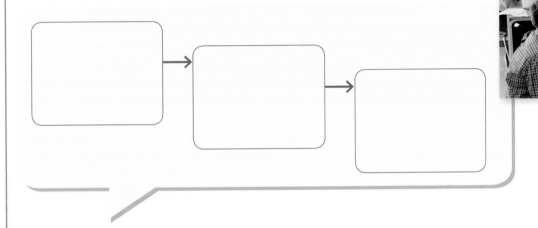

2. Close your book. Work in groups. Describe your place to your group. Ask your partners questions about their places.

Step 3 REPORT

Write notes about your partners' places. Then write two sentences about the place you want to visit.

	Name of place	Interesting details
Partner 1		
Partner 2		

Step 4 REFLECT

Checklist

Check (✓) the things you learned in Chapter 5.

- ○ I learned language to describe a place outdoors.
- ○ I understood a news story about moss tours in Japan.
- ○ I described an interesting place to visit in my city.

Discussion Question

Is it important to spend time in nature? Why or why not?

- Use the present progressive
- Listen for interjections
- Recognize the present progressive with *not*

- Listen for effects with *so*
- Practice linking with plural *-s*
- Give directions to a local place

▲ VOCABULARY ▶ Oxford 2000 🔑 words to talk about getting around the city

Learn Words

🔊 **A. Label each picture with the correct word. Then listen and repeat the words and phrases.**

| advice | bridge | street | ~~directions~~ | painting | rain | taxi | train |

1.
asking for _____directions_____

2.
crossing the _____

3.
taking the _____

4.
getting travel _____

5.
sitting in a _____

6.
standing on the _____

7.
looking at a _____

8.
walking in the _____

Grammar Note

The present progressive

🔊 Speakers use the present progressive to talk about actions that are happening right now. Listen to the examples.

> A: Where **are you going**?
>
> B: **I'm going** to the store. Do you want to come with me?

🔊 Use *am/is/are + ing* to form the present progressive. When speakers use the present progressive, they often use contractions with the subject. Listen to the examples.

> **She's coming** with us.   **We're looking** for a restaurant.
>
> **They're taking** the bus.

🔊 To ask questions, speakers use *am/is/are* before the subject. Listen to the examples.

> **Are you taking** the train?   What **is he looking** at?

🔊 **B. Listen and repeat.**

A	B
1. Are you listening?	Yes, I'm listening.
2. Are they coming?	Yes, they're coming.
3. Is it raining?	Yes, it's raining.
4. Where are we going?	We're going to work.
5. Where is she walking?	She's walking home.
6. When is he coming?	He's coming later.

C. Work with a partner. Partner A asks a question from Activity B. Partner B gives the correct response. Then partners switch roles.

🔊 **D. Listen to each statement. Check (✓) the words you hear.**

1. ☐ I try…   ✓ I'm trying…

2. ☐ They walk…   ☐ They're walking…

3. ☐ She looks…   ☐ She's looking….

4. ☐ It takes…   ☐ It's taking…

5. ☐ We look…   ☐ We're looking…

Learn Phrases

🔊 **A. Match each phrase to the correct picture. Then listen and repeat.**

a map of the city	**pay attention to** the time
follow the route for walkers	**remember stuff** to do
get help from a friend	**use GPS** on my phone
having **a fun adventure**	watch **local artists**

1.

2.

3.

4.

5.

6.

7.

8.

B. Listen to each conversation. Circle the correct answer.

1. They're   *using GPS.*   *using a map.*

2. She's not paying attention   *to the rain.*   *to the route.*

3. The store sells a lot of   *fun stuff.*   *local stuff.*

4. She is going to   *follow the cars.*   *follow the map.*

5. He wants   *a local route.*   *a local train.*

C. Add words to make new phrases.

1. buy stuff for   my friends

                 my family _____

2. watch local   games

                _____

3. get help from   my parents

                _____

4. have a fun   time

                _____

5. remember people's   names

                _____

6. follow   the rules

                _____

D. Work with a partner. Ask and answer the questions.

Partner A	Partner B
1. Are you having fun?	2. Are you remembering stuff from class?
3. Are you listening closely to the teacher?	4. Are you working hard?
5. Are you learning a lot in school?	6. Are you learning new words?

GO ONLINE for more practice

▲▲ LISTENING

CONVERSATION

🔊 **A. Listen to the conversation. Then check (✓) the relationship of the speakers.**

☐ a teacher and a student   ☐ two friends   ☐ a tourist and a local person

🔊 **B. Listen to the conversation again. Number the events in the correct order.**

_____ He learns about a café.   _____ He gets a taxi.   _____ He asks for directions.

Listening Strategy

Listening for interjections

🔊 Speakers use interjections to express how they feel. Listen to the examples.

Interjection	Meaning
A: *The bus station is on the corner.* B: **OK. Thanks!**	**OK** = I understand. **Thanks!** = I'm thankful.
A: *There's a nice park on Smith Street.* B: **Oh,** *the park. Yes, thanks!*	**Oh** = I'm thinking. / I know about that.
A: *You'll like the people there.* B: **Great!**	**Great!** = That's interesting. / I'm happy.

GO ONLINE
for more
practice

🔊 **C. Listen to the conversation again. Write the interjections you hear.**

A: Excuse me. Are you from here? I'm looking for the art museum.

B: _____, the art museum. Sure. Are you taking the train?

A: No. I'm walking.

B: _____. So, cross the street and walk down Marshall. Cross the bridge, and the museum will be on the corner of Marshall and Smith.

A: _____! Thanks.

B: Sure. And by the way, there's a great café by the museum. It has good food.

A: _____, really?

B: Yes. The name is Lily's Bistro. It's a local place. And it has unusual art on the walls. The paintings are by local artists. It's really interesting.

A: _____. Well, thanks!

B: No problem. Just be careful. It's starting to rain.

Sounds of English

The present progressive with *not*

When speakers use the present progressive, they use *not* to make a statement negative. Speakers often reduce *is not* to *isn't* and *are not* to *aren't* in the present progressive. Listen to the examples.

> My phone **isn't** working. Can I use your phone?
>
> They **aren't** coming today. They're coming tomorrow.

When speakers correct information, they often contract the verb *be* and stress *not*. Listen to the examples.

> **I'm not** taking a taxi. I'm taking the bus.
>
> **We're not** going to the store now. We're going later.

D. Listen to each statement. Check (✓) the phrase you hear.

	A		B
1.	☐ He's not going.	✓	He isn't going.
2.	☐ They're not trying.	☐	They aren't trying.
3.	☐ It's not working.	☐	It isn't working.
4.	☐ She's not driving.	☐	She isn't driving.
5.	☐ You're not looking.	☐	You aren't looking.
6.	☐ We're not walking.	☐	We aren't walking.

E. Listen and underline the words that are stressed. Then listen again and check your answers.

1. A: Are you walking?
   B: I'm not walking. I'm driving.

2. A: Is it raining?
   B: No, it's not raining.

3. A: Are they going?
   B: They're not going. They're staying.

4. A: Are we leaving now?
   B: No, we're not leaving until later.

5. A: Are you working right now?
   B: I'm not working. I'm watching a movie.

6. A: Is the bus coming?
   B: It's not coming. Let's take a taxi.

Chant

GO ONLINE for the Chapter 6 Vocabulary & Grammar Chant

F. Practice the conversations in Activity E with a partner.

ACADEMIC LISTENING

A. Use *always, sometimes,* or *never* to complete each statement about you. Then compare with a partner.

1. I _____ use GPS when I'm driving.

2. I _____ use a paper map when I travel to other countries.

3. I _____ get lost in new places.

4. I _____ give people bad directions.

5. I _____ remember the routes I take.

B. Listen to the first section. Circle the correct answers.

1. *Mark   Mallory*   likes to use paper maps.

2. *Mark   Mallory*   uses GPS.

3. *Map users   GPS users*   give better directions.

Listening Strategy

Listening for effects with *so*

Speakers use *so* to signal an effect. Listen to the example.

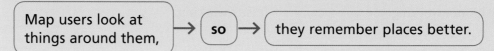

Map users look at things around them, → **so** → they remember places better.

GO ONLINE
for more
practice

C. Listen to the second section. Match the contrasting ideas.

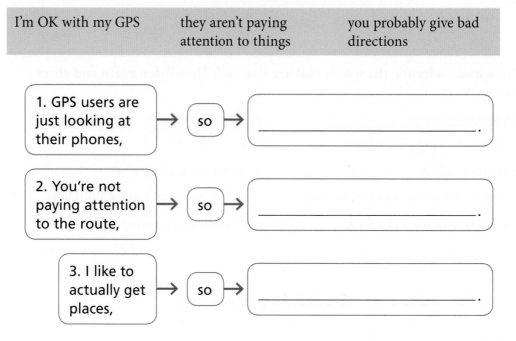

I'm OK with my GPS	they aren't paying attention to things	you probably give bad directions

1. GPS users are just looking at their phones, → **so** → _____.

2. You're not paying attention to the route, → **so** → _____.

3. I like to actually get places, → **so** → _____.

D. Listen to the conversation again. Ask and answer the questions with a partner.

Partner A	Partner B
1. Who is terrible at giving directions?	2. Why does Mallory prefer to use GPS?
3. What do map users pay attention to?	4. What do GPS users pay attention to?
5. Why do map users have more adventures?	6. Why do GPS users give bad directions?

Discuss the Ideas

E. Work in small groups. Use the phrases in the chart and your own ideas to discuss other differences between map users and GPS users.

Map users...	get lost more easily have better adventures make better plans relax more	but	GPS users...
GPS users...	save money save time talk to more people worry more		map users...

> GPS users save time, but map users have better adventures.

F. Work with a partner. Talk about how you get to new places.

Partner A	Partner B
I use a GPS in my car. I look at a map before I go. Sometimes I get lost, but that's OK. When I walk, I don't like to look at my phone.	Me too! I am the same way! Oh, really? I'm different. I never/ always... Yeah, it can be fun to... Interesting! Do you ever get lost?

▲▲▲ SPEAKING

Speaking Task Giving directions to a local place

Step 1 PREPARE

Pronunciation Skill

Linking with plural -s

◀)) Speakers add an -s on a noun to make it plural. The plural -s can have three different sounds. Listen to the examples.

Sounds like /s/	Sounds like /z/	Sounds like /ɪz/
artists	*cities*	*beaches*
maps	*directions*	*buses*
rocks	*paintings*	*places*

Speakers often link the plural -s with words that begin with vowels. Listen to the examples.

The streets are getting busier. → *The street-**sar** getting busier.*

There are two buildings on the corner. → *There are two building-**zon** the corner.*

GO ONLINE
for more
practice

◀)) **A. Listen and repeat the phrases.**

A	B
1. my place	my places
2. a busy road	busy roads
3. the bus	the buses
4. on campus	on campuses
5. by the building	by the buildings

 B. Practice with a partner. Partner A says a phrase from Activity A. Partner B says the letter of the correct column. Then partners switch roles.

◀)) **C. Listen and repeat.**

1. cars	cars are	Cars are expensive.
2. flowers	flowers are	Flowers are colorful.
3. artists	artists are	Artists are different.
4. trains	trains are	Trains are noisy.

D. Work in two groups. Group 1 listens and repeats the statements from column A. Group 2 listens and repeats the statements from column B.

A	B
1. Why are we standing here?	Because the buses are running late.
2. There are many local artists in this neighborhood.	Really? That's cool.
3. It's raining very hard right now!	That's why the streets are so bad.
4. There are too many cars on the street.	Yes. Let's wait.
5. Where's Marshall Street?	You'll see it. There are apartments on the corner.
6. What do you like paintings of?	I like nature paintings a lot.

E. Listen. Complete each conversation with a phrase from the box.

~~clothes are~~	plans are	rooms are	stores are	videos are

1. A: Those _____clothes are_____ nice.

   B: They are! Let's go inside.

2. A: I think the _____ open until 10.

   B: OK. Let me check online.

3. A: His _____ cool.

   B: I like his music videos the best.

4. A: Our _____ to walk downtown and eat lunch.

   B: That sounds good. It's a nice day for it.

5. A: This is a nice apartment.

   B: Yes, but the _____ small.

GO ONLINE
to practice the
conversation

F. Work with a partner. Practice the conversations in Activity E.

G. Work with a partner. Partner A says a sentence. Partner B points to the correct sentence. Then partners switch roles.

1. What street can I take?	What streets can I take?
2. It's close to the store.	It's close to the stores.
3. I need direction.	I need directions.
4. What place do you know?	What places do you know?
5. It's near the bus.	It's near the buses.
6. The train can be late.	The trains can be late.

Step 2 SPEAK

A. Work with a partner. Think about popular places in your city. List the names of the places in the chart.

Places	Names
a historic neighborhood	Chinatown
a famous street	
an interesting store	
a good restaurant	

B. Look at your list in Activity A. Tell your partner why you like each place. What can people do there? What can they see?

Speaking Skill

The for unique nouns

Speakers use *the* to talk about specific people, places, and things. *The* often means "the only one(s)." Listen to the examples.

the + noun	Meaning
*I like **the people** here.*	*The* means only the people at that place.
*I'm going to **the art museum.***	*The* means there is only one art museum.
***The food** at Lily's is good.*	*The* means only Lily's makes the food.

Word Partners

on the left
on the right
on the corner
on the street
on (the) campus

GO ONLINE to practice word partners

C. Work with a partner. Ask and answer the questions about your school.

Partner A	Partner B
1. Where's the library?	2. Where's the computer lab?
3. Does the cafeteria have healthy food?	4. Is the campus big or small?
5. When does the campus close?	6. Does the food at the school taste good?
7. Where do the students have fun?	8. When does the library open?

Speaking Task

Giving directions to a local place

1. Choose a popular place in your city. Create a role-play between a tourist and a local. Use ideas in the flow chart.

> Excuse me, where is...
> How do you get to...
> Hello, I am trying to find...

> It's near here. You can walk.
> You can take a bus. The bus stop is over there.
> It's pretty far. Maybe take a car or a taxi.

> Thank you!
> Great, we'll try that.
> Actually, we prefer...

> You'll like...
> You can...
> Try to see the...
> Check out the... It's interesting.

2. Close your book. Practice your role-play with a partner.

3. Work with another pair. Perform your role-plays for one another.

Step 3 REPORT

Complete the following sentences to write about the role-play you watched.

The tourist wants to go to _____.

The local tells the tourist to _____.

The tourist decides to _____.

The local advises the tourist to _____.

Step 4 REFLECT

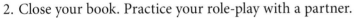

Checklist

Check (✓) the things you learned in Chapter 6.

○ I learned language to describe how to get around the city.

○ I understood radio DJs chat about differences between GPS and maps users.

○ I participated in a role-play between a tourist and a local.

Discussion Question

Do you like talking to local people when you travel?

Look at the word bank for Unit 2. Check (✓) the words you know. Circle the words you want to learn better.

OXFORD 2000 🔑

Adjectives	Nouns		Verbs
bright	advice	house	cost
close	animal	kind	cross
comfortable	apartment	light	feel
dark	area	money	grow
far	artist	mountain	put
green	bedroom	painting	ride
high	bridge	path	save
local	bus	picture	sit
pretty	color	plant	stand
proud	corner	rain	stay
quick	detail	rock	take
same	direction	street	think
simple	flower	tour	travel
strange	forest	train	wait
tall	furniture	wall	walk
wild	help	window	
	hotel		

PRACTICE WITH THE OXFORD 2000 🔑

A. Use the chart. Match adjectives with nouns.

1. _____a pretty flower_____   2. _____

3. _____   4. _____

5. _____   6. _____

B. Use the chart. Match verbs with nouns.

1. _____take advice_____   2. _____

3. _____   4. _____

5. _____   6. _____

C. Use the chart. Match verbs with adjective noun partners.

1. _____cross local streets_____   2. _____

3. _____   4. _____

5. _____   6. _____

UNIT **3** Products

CHAPTER **7**   ## Is That Your Best Price?

▲ **VOCABULARY**
- Oxford 2000 🔑 words to talk about bargains

▲▲ **LISTENING**
- Listening for -ty/-teen in prices
- Listening for pronouns

▲▲▲ **SPEAKING**
- Practicing pronoun reductions
- Bargaining about prices

CHAPTER **8**   ## How Do You Like That Bike?

▲ **VOCABULARY**
- Oxford 2000 🔑 words to talk about products

▲▲ **LISTENING**
- Listening for encouragement
- Listening to learn how people use something

▲▲▲ **SPEAKING**
- Practicing words with the /p/ sound
- Reviewing a product and its features

CHAPTER **9**   ## Who Gave It to You?

▲ **VOCABULARY**
- Oxford 2000 🔑 words to talk about special gifts

▲▲ **LISTENING**
- Listening for strong feelings with *really*
- Listening for past and present time signals

▲▲▲ **SPEAKING**
- Practicing -*ed* endings
- Telling about a special possession

UNIT WRAP UP   ## Extend Your Skills

- Use *this/these* and *that/those*
- Listen for *-ty/-teen* in prices
- Recognize linking of *these/those* with *are*

- Listen for pronouns
- Practice pronoun reductions
- Bargain about prices

▲ VOCABULARY ▶ Oxford 2000 🔑 words to talk about bargains

Learn Words

🔊 **A. Label each picture with the correct word. Then listen and repeat the words and phrases.**

| change | customers | deal | joke | market | shirts | shoes | ~~watch~~ |

1.

choose a _____watch_____

2.

sell _____

3.

give _____

4.

shop at an outdoor _____

5.

find a good _____ on clothes

6.

talk to _____ online

7.

buy women's _____

8.

read a funny _____

Grammar Note

This, *these*, *that*, and *those*

🔊 Use *this* + a singular noun to talk about something that is close to you. Use *these* before plural nouns. Listen to the examples.

> A: *Do you like* **these** *shoes?*
>
> B: *Not really, but I like* **this** *shirt a lot. I think I'll try it on.*

🔊 Use *that* or *those* + noun for something that is farther away. Listen to the example.

> A: **Those** *buildings look old.*
>
> B: *They do. But* **that** *building looks modern.*

🔊 **B. Listen and repeat.**

A	B
1. this watch	these watches
2. this store	these stores
3. this price	these prices
4. that shoe	those shoes
5. that customer	those customers
6. that painting	those paintings

C. Work with a partner. Partner A says the phrase from column A in Activity B. Partner B says the phrase from column B. Then partners switch roles.

🔊 **D. Listen to each statement. Check (✓) the statement you hear.**

1. [✓] This book is great.   [ ] These books are great.

2. [ ] This plan will work.   [ ] These plans will work.

3. [ ] I like this bag.   [ ] I like these bags.

4. [ ] That idea is good.   [ ] Those ideas are good.

5. [ ] That shop sells clothes.   [ ] Those shops sell clothes.

6. [ ] I love that tree.   [ ] I love those trees.

E. Work with a partner. Partner A says a statement from Activity D. Partner B repeats the statement. Then partners switch roles.

Learn Phrases

🔊 **A. Match each phrase to the correct picture. Then listen and repeat.**

bargain for a lower price on clothes	**different products** for women
follow the rules of the city	**higher prices** for homes
pay cash for food	try to **choose the best fruit**
two pairs of shoes	**walk away from** the store

1.

2.

3.

4.

5.

6.

7.

8.

B. Listen to each conversation. Circle the correct answer.

1. The man is   *paying cash.*   *getting change.*

2. The customer will buy   *two pairs of shoes.*   *two kinds of watches.*

3. The speaker usually shops   *at outdoor markets.*   *at expensive stores.*

4. The store sells   *products for men.*   *products for women.*

5. The customer wants   *to bargain.*   *to walk away.*

C. Circle two words that pair with the noun or phrase.

1. *bargain*   *buy*   *sell*   products

2. *read*   *make*   *shop*   the rules

3. *wait*   *hear*   *tell*   a joke

4. *find*   *bargain*   *talk*   with customers

5. *choose*   *cost*   *wear*   shoes

6. *save*   *swim*   *shop*   at stores

D. Read each question. Circle your answer. Then ask and answer the questions with a partner.

1. How do you shop?   *I compare prices.*   *I compare products.*   *I ask questions about products.*

2. Where do you shop?   *I visit different stores.*   *I go to outdoor markets.*   *I shop online.*

3. What do you buy?   *I buy things I like.*   *I buy things I need.*   *I buy the best products I can.*

4. How do you save?   *I try to bargain.*   *I buy things on sale.*   *I buy simpler products.*

5. How do you bargain?   *I pay cash.*   *I ask for the best price.*   *I don't really bargain.*

How do you shop?

I compare prices.

Where do you shop?

I shop online.

GO ONLINE
for more
practice

▲▲ LISTENING

CONVERSATION

🔊 **A. Listen to the conversation. What does the shopper buy? Circle the correct answer.**

an expensive shirt   an expensive table   an expensive watch

🔊 **B. Listen to the conversation again. Circle the correct answer to complete each statement.**

1. The customer is at   *a grocery store.   a clothing store.*

2. The customer   *pays full price.   asks for a lower price.*

3. The customer   *walks away.   gets change.*

Listening Strategy

Listening for *-ty/-teen* in prices

🔊 Some prices in English sound similar. To hear the difference, listen for the stress. Prices that end in *-ty* have stress on the first syllable. Prices that end in *-teen* have stress on both syllables. Listen to the examples.

-ty		*-teen*	
$30	***thir*ty dollars**	$13	thirteen dollars
$40	***for*ty dollars**	$14	fourteen dollars
$50	***fif*ty dollars**	$15	fifteen dollars

GO ONLINE
for more
practice

🔊 **C. Listen to the conversation again. Circle the prices you hear.**

A: Hello. Can I help you?

B: Yes, we're looking at these shirts. How much are they?

A: Those are $20. Buy five or more, and they're $18 / $80.   Do you like them?

B: Yes, they're nice. And what about those watches?

A: Those are $15 / $50.   But we have these watches, too. They're cheaper.

B: Hmm…I prefer the more expensive ones. Can you go lower on the price?

A: Well, for you, I can do $40 / $14.

B: Hmm…that's a little high. How about $13 / $30?   And I pay cash?

A: For cash, I can do $35.

B: OK. It's a deal. Here's $50 / $15.

A: OK, and here's your change. That's $50 / $15.

Linking of *these/those* with *are*

When speakers talk quickly, they often link *these* and *those* with *are*. The link sounds like "zer." Listen to the examples.

zer
These are cheap shoes. → *These're cheap shoes.*

zer
Those are more expensive. → *Those're more expensive.*

D. Listen and repeat.

A	B
1. These are big.	Those are small.
2. These are mine.	Those are yours.
3. These are new.	Those are old.
4. These are light.	Those are dark.
5. These are good.	Those are bad.

E. Listen to each statement. Check (✓) the linked phrase you hear.

A | B

1. ☐ These are… ✓ Those are…

2. ☐ These are… ☐ Those are…

3. ☐ These are… ☐ Those are…

4. ☐ These are… ☐ Those are…

5. ☐ These are… ☐ Those are…

F. Listen to each conversation. Write *These are* or *Those are*.

1. A: ___Those are___ nice watches.
   B: Which ones?

2. A: _____ for sale, right?
   B: Yes, they are.

3. A: _____ my new shoes.
   B: Oh, they're nice!

4. A: _____ great deals!
   B: I know!

5. A: Why can't we do that?
   B: _____ the rules.
      That's why.

6. A: _____ for you.
   B: Oh, thank you! I love flowers!

Chant

GO ONLINE for the Chapter 7 Vocabulary & Grammar Chant

A. Work with a partner. Describe the two places. Make statements with the phrases in the box.

are more expensive	are more interesting
have better deals	sell newer products
sell nicer things	

Stores

Outdoor markets

B. Listen to the first section. Where do people get better deals? Circle the correct answer.

at stores   *at schools*   *at outdoor markets*

C. Listen to whole interview. Check (✓) the people that each statement describes.

	Customers	Sellers
1. They ask for the best price.		
2. They walk away.		
3. They make funny jokes.		

Listening Strategy

Listening for pronouns

Speakers use pronouns to replace nouns. Listen to the examples.

> A: So, you say <u>people</u> get better deals at outdoor markets…why?
>
> B: Well, it's because **they** can bargain.
>
> A: What does <u>the seller</u> say?
>
> B: **He** tells <u>the woman</u> $50. And **she** says, "How about $15?"

GO ONLINE
for more
practice

D. Match the people to the correct pronouns. Then listen and check your answers.

people in Asia	the customer and seller
the seller	these shoes
this woman	

_____ 1. They're good bargainers.

_____ 2. She's shopping.

_____ 3. But they're expensive.

_____ 4. He says no.

_____ 5. They laugh.

E. Listen to the interview again. Then ask and answer the questions with a partner.

Partner A	Partner B
1. Where do people get better deals? 3. When does the woman walk away? 5. What do customers need to do?	2. Where do people bargain all the time? 4. Why is it like a game? 6. What do sellers need to do?

Discuss the Ideas

F. Work with a partner. Describe outdoor markets or local shops. Use the words from the chart and your own ideas.

Partner A	Partner B
The farmer's market is fun. I like the local shops. I always save money at… I always go to…	Yeah, you can bargain there, and… Oh, but I disagree with the prices! Yes, but do you have to pay cash? Really? Do you get better…there?

▲▲▲ SPEAKING

Speaking Task Bargaining about prices

Step 1 PREPARE

Pronunciation Skill

Pronoun reductions

◀ When speakers talk quickly, they often reduce the pronouns *him*, *her*, and *them* after verbs. Listen to the examples.

> *I don't know him.* → *I don't know /im.*
>
> *Can you see her?* → *Can you see /er?*
>
> *Do you sell them?* → *Do you sell /em?*

◀ When speakers reduce *him*, *her*, or *them*, they usually link it with a verb. Listen to the examples.

> *I want them.* → *I want /em.*
>
> *I see him.* → *I see /im.*
>
> *I know her.* → *I know /er.*

GO ONLINE
for more
practice

◀ **A. Listen and repeat.**

A	B
1. I'll buy them.	I'll buy /em.
2. I'll call her.	I'll call /er.
3. Can we visit him?	Can we visit /im?
4. Let's clean them.	Let's clean /em.
5. They can't watch her.	They can't watch /er.

◀ **B. Listen to each statement. Check (✓) the phrase the speaker links.**

	A		B
1.	☐ know them	✓	like them
2.	☐ have them	☐	sell them
3.	☐ visit him	☐	visit them
4.	☐ call him	☐	call her

C. Listen and use the phrases from the box to complete the conversation.

| ask her | have them | like them | need them | see him | try them |

A: Those shoes are nice. Where's the seller?

B: I don't _____ see him _____.

A: What about that woman? Does she work here?

B: Let's _____.

A: Excuse me. Do you work here? I'm looking at these shoes.

C: Do you want to _____? I _____ in blue, too. See those?

A: Oh, yes. I _____ in blue. How much?

C: They're $30.

A: Will you take $50 for two pairs? I _____ for work.

C: It's a deal.

A: Great. Here's $50.

C: Thanks. Have a nice day.

B: Have a good one!

GO ONLINE to practice the conversation

D. Work with two partners. Practice the conversation in Activity C.

E. Work with a partner. Partner A asks a question. Partner B answers correctly. Then partners switch roles.

1. a. Can you see her?   No, she's too far away.
   b. Can you see them?   Yes, they're over there.

2. a. Do you want them?   Yes, I do.
   b. Do you need them?   No, I don't.

3. a. Let's ask her.   OK. I'll talk to her.
   b. Let's ask him.   Do you want to call him?

4. a. I want to buy them.   They're $10.
   b. I want to try them.   What color do you want?

5. a. I think I know him.   Who? Him? From where?
   b. I think I know them.   How do you know them?

6. a. I'll take them.   Great!
   b. I'll make them.   Do you need help?

A. Work with a partner. Choose roles. Then use the questions to discuss your role-play.

Customer	Seller
Who is the customer?	Who is the seller?
What are you looking at?	What product(s) are you selling?
What do you want to buy?	What is your high price?
How much will you pay?	What's your best price?

Speaking Skill

Asking for a lower price

There are several expressions speakers use to bargain for a lower price. Listen to the examples.

Can you go lower on the price?   *What's your best price?*

Can you go any lower?   *How low can you go?*

How about $30?   *Will you take $20?*

B. Listen and complete each conversation with the question you hear.

1. A: _____
   B: Sorry, I can't go lower than $15.

2. A: _____
   B: My best price? For you, $17.

3. A: _____
   B: I can go as low as $10, but no lower.

4. A: Those watches are $30. They're from Japan.
   B: _____

5. A: _____
   B: $30 is too low. I can do $35.

6. A: _____
   B: I can when you buy two.

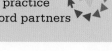

Word Partners

a little big

a little expensive

a little high

a little low

a little small

GO ONLINE
to practice
word partners

C. Practice the conversations in Activity B with a partner.

Speaking Task

Bargaining about prices

1. Work with a partner. Use the chart to help you create two role-plays. In one, you are the buyer. In the other, you are the seller.

Customer	Seller
Tell me about that… I'm interested in these…	Of course, it's a great… Oh these, these are…
How much is it? How much are they?	It's a great deal… Those…? You can have them for…
What's your best price? Can you go any lower?	I can sell it to you for… How about…?
OK, I'll take it. Hmm…I'll walk away this time.	Great! OK.

2. Work with another pair. Perform your role-plays for one another.

Step 3 REPORT

Complete the report with information from the role-plays.

Product			
Seller			
Price			
Sale? Yes or No			

Step 4 REFLECT

Checklist

Check (✓) the things you learned in Chapter 7.

○ I learned language about buying and selling products.

○ I understood a news story about how people bargain at outdoor markets.

○ I participated in a role-play between a customer and a seller.

Discussion Question

How do you find the best bargains?

- Use *make* with adjectives and verbs
- Listen for encouragement
- Recognize linking of *is* with vowel sounds
- Listen to learn how people use something
- Practice words with the /p/ sound
- Review a product and its features

▲ VOCABULARY ▶ Oxford 2000 ✎ words to talk about products

Learn Words

🔊 **A. Label each picture with the correct word. Then listen and repeat the words and phrases.**

backpack	camera	car	glasses	knife	jacket	motorcycle	size

1.

the perfect _____*size*_____

2.

a kitchen _____

3.

a warm _____

4.

a sports _____

5.

a fast _____

6.

a travel _____

7.

a video _____

8.

cool _____

Grammar Note

Make with adjectives and verbs

Speakers use *make* + a noun or pronoun with adjectives and verbs to show the effects of something. Listen to the examples.

Make with adjectives	*Make* with verbs
I like my new camera. It **makes** <u>me</u> happy.	My friends tell jokes. They **make** <u>me</u> laugh.
My new car **makes** <u>me</u> popular.	My new glasses **make** <u>me</u> look cool.
Riding a motorcycle **makes** <u>me</u> nervous.	This app **makes** <u>me</u> exercise.

B. Listen and repeat each question and answer.

Question	Answer
1. How does your bicycle make you feel?	It makes me happy.
2. How do you like that backpack?	A lot! It makes me want to travel.
3. Do you like your car?	Yes! It makes me feel successful.
4. Does your camera take good pictures?	Yes, it makes them look beautiful!
5. How do you like that motorcycle?	Oh, it makes my life exciting.
6. Do the knives make your work easier?	No, they don't. They make me nervous!

C. Practice asking and answering the questions in Activity B with a partner. Then switch roles.

D. Work with a partner. Use the words in the chart and your own ideas to ask and answer questions.

Partner A			Partner B		Partner A
How does	cooking driving a car listening to music riding a motorcycle shopping texting friends	make you feel?	It makes me feel	good. excited. happy. nervous.	That's good. That's too bad.

How does riding a motorcycle make you feel?

It makes me feel nervous.

Oh, that's too bad. I love it.

Learn Phrases

🔊 **A. Match each phrase to the correct picture. Then listen and repeat.**

a camera with **special features**	an app to **communicate with friends**
do **a customer review** of a product	doesn't have **a reliable car**
have a problem with my laptop	**have experience** in sports
recommend products to customers	use a knife to **chop vegetables**

1.

_____

2.

_____

3.

_____

4.

_____

5.

_____

6.

_____

7.

_____

8.

_____

B. Listen to each conversation. Circle the product.

1. glasses   (shoes)
2. phone   camera
3. motorcycle   car
4. television   laptop
5. his knives   his furniture
6. apartment   computer

C. Circle two words that pair with the noun.

1. *fast*   *nervous*   *reliable*   computer
2. *size*   *product*   *restaurant*   review
3. *warm*   *expensive*   *special*   knife
4 *simple*   *interesting* *perfect*   problem
5. *local*   *cheap*   *used*   jacket
6. *cool*   *proud*   *popular*   features

D. Complete the sentences with the names of things you have.

1. My _____ is perfect for me.
2. My _____ has a lot of great features.
3. I usually have a good experience with my _____.
4. I know a lot about _____.
5. Buying my _____ was a good idea.
6. Sometimes I have problems with my _____.

E. Work with a partner. Close your books. Tell your partner about things you have. Ask your partner about things he or she has.

My apartment is perfect for me.

Really? Why do you like it?

It's a good size, and it's in a great neighborhood.

GO ONLINE
for more
practice

▲▲ LISTENING

CONVERSATION

🔊 **A. Listen to the conversation. What are they talking about? Circle the correct answer.**

a class assignment   a new cooking show on the Internet   an idea for a restaurant review

🔊 **B. Listen to the conversation again. Circle the correct answers.**

1. Ana helps Jaime by   *cooking for him.*   *helping him make a decision.*

2. Jaime is taking   *a business class.*   *a cooking class.*

3. Jaime decides to make a video about   *his knives.*   *his apartment.*

Listening Strategy

Listening for encouragement

🔊 Friends often try to help each other when it's hard to make decisions. This encouragement helps the other person feel good. Listen to the examples.

Asking for encouragement	**Giving encouragement**
Am I making a mistake?	*No, I think you'll be just fine.*
Am I doing the right thing?	*Of course! It's something you love, right?*
Don't you think that's strange?	*No, not at all.*
Are you sure it's a good idea?	*Yes, it'll be great!*

GO ONLINE
for more
practice

 C. Work with a partner. Practice the questions and answers in the Listening Strategy box.

🔊 **D. Listen to the conversation again. Then check (✓) the correct answers.**

1. Jaime says he likes cooking. What does Ana say?

☐ a. That's a good start. You're a great cook.

☐ b. That's something to think about.

2. Jaime is nervous that the idea is strange. What does Ana say?

☐ a. Don't worry about that! Everybody has strange ideas.

☐ b. No, not at all. It's something you love, right?

3. Jaime finally decides on his topic. What does Ana say?

☐ a. I guess that'll work.

☐ b. It'll be great! I want to see it.

Sounds of English

Linking of *is* with vowel sounds

🔊 When people use *is* before a vowel sound, the vowel sound links to the *s*. Listen to the examples.

It is a business class. → *It's a business class.*

It is easy to use. → *It's easy to use.*

He is in the kitchen. → *He's in the kitchen.*

🔊 **E. Mark each place the *s* and vowel sound should be linked. Then listen and repeat.**

A	B	A
1. It's easy.	What's easy?	The book's easy.
2. It's important.	What's important?	The class is important.
3. It's in the car.	What's in the car?	My backpack's in the car.
4. It's an app.	What's an app?	The game's an app.
5. It's a problem.	What's a problem?	The color is a problem.
6. It's on the desk.	What's on the desk?	The jacket's on the desk.

F. Work with a partner. Use the words in the chart and your own ideas to ask and answer questions.

Partner A	Partner B	
What is it?	It's	an apartment.
		an app.
		a car.
		a computer.
		a jacket.
		a knife.
		a phone.

Partner A	Partner B
Oh, it's a/an….	Yes, that's right.
	No, it's a/an…

Chant

GO ONLINE for the Chapter 8 Vocabulary & Grammar Chant

ACADEMIC LISTENING

A. Check (✓) the questions you ask when you want to buy something.

☐ Is it expensive? ☐ Is it reliable?

☐ How do you use it? ☐ What are the features?

☐ What are the problems with it? ☐ What do people like about it?

B. Work as a group to answer the questions. Share your results with the class.

1. Do you read customer reviews to learn about products? Why or why not? _____

_____

2. Do you post customer reviews online? Why or why not? _____

_____

C. Listen to the introduction. Where are the speakers? Circle the correct answer.

at a store   *in a business class*   *in an apartment*

D. Listen to the discussion. Write the product that each person talks about.

Person	Product
Juan	
Lena	
Constantine	

Listening Strategy

Listening to learn how people use something

To talk about a product's features, people often use the word *use* with an object and *to* + verb. Listen to the examples.

Singular nouns	**Plural nouns**
I **use** my backpack **to carry** food.	I **use** my knives **to cut** fruit.
I **use** my phone **to play** games.	I **use** apps **to communicate**.

GO ONLINE
for more
practice

E. Listen to each section and complete the statements.

1. Juan uses his ____phone____ to _____ and

   _____.

2. Lena uses her _____ to _____ and

   _____.

3. Constantine uses his _____ to _____.

F. Listen to the introduction and discussion again. Then ask and answer the questions with a partner.

Partner A	Partner B
1. What class are the students taking? 3. How does Juan use his phone? 5. When does Lena use her backpack?	2. What is their assignment? 4. Why does Lena like her backpack? 6. Why does Constantine want a new motorcycle?

Discuss the Ideas

G. Work with a partner. Use the words in the chart and your own ideas to talk about things you own.

Partner A		Partner B
Do you have a good Do you have a reliable	bicycle? car? computer? laptop? motorcycle? phone?	Yes, I do. Yeah, it's OK, I guess.

Partner A	Partner B	
How do you use it? Tell me about it.	I use it to	communicate. go to school. look for information. play games. travel. watch movies.

Speaking Task Reviewing a product and its features

Step 1 PREPARE

Pronunciation Skill

Words with the /p/ sound

🔊 The sound /p/ appears in the beginning, middle, and end of many words. Listen to the examples.

Beginning	Middle	End
perfect	back**p**ack	a**pp**
place	ex**p**ensive	cho**p**
s**p**ecial	im**p**ortant	sho**p**

GO ONLINE
for more
practice

🔊 **A. Listen to the phrases. Check (✓) *same* if you hear the same phrase. Check (✓) *different* if the phrases are different.**

1. ☐ same   ✓ different

2. ☐ same   ☐ different

3. ☐ same   ☐ different

4. ☐ same   ☐ different

5. ☐ same   ☐ different

6. ☐ same   ☐ different

🔊 **B. Listen and repeat.**

1. place	path	plan
2. shop	chop	stop
3. people	product	prefer
4. sports	special	spend
5. expensive	apartment	important
6. happy	simple	expert

C. Listen. Complete the conversation with the words from the box.

~~apartment~~   campus   expensive   perfect   places   prefer   problems   spend

Tai: I moved to an _____apartment_____ off campus, and now I need to get
to school every day.

Viktor: You're going to need a bicycle or something.

Tai: Actually, I _____ a motorcycle, but they're more
_____.

Victor: Right. A motorcycle is fun, but are you sure you need it? I have a bicycle,
and I love it. I can ride it right onto _____.

Tai: That's good. How do you like your bike?

Victor: It's a mountain bike, so it's not fast, but it's _____ for me. I can
use it to go more _____ in nature.

Tai: Does it have any _____?

Victor: No, not really. I'm happy with it.

Tai: Well, I can't _____ a lot of money right now.

Victor: Then I recommend a city bike. It's simpler.

Tai: OK, I'll think about it.

GO ONLINE
to practice the
conversation

D. Practice the conversation in Activity C with a partner.

E. Work with a partner. Partner A asks a question. Partner B answers correctly. Then partners switch roles.

1. a. Where is a good place to shop for vegetables?   At the store.
   b. Where is a good space to chop vegetables?   In the kitchen.

2. a. It's a perfect size.   Yes, it fits well.
   b. It's a special price.   Good, you can buy it.

3. a. It's a perfect backpack.   I'm glad you like it.
   b. I prefer that backpack.   Then don't buy this one.

4. a. You can compare products online.   Good idea. I want to compare prices, too.
   b. You can compare glasses online.   Yes, there are many different kinds of glasses?

5. a. It's an expensive watch.   I know.
   b. How expensive is that watch?   It's very expensive.

A. Write four products you have in the chart. Write two you like and two you don't like.

I like my...		
I don't like my...		

B. Work with a partner. Tell your partner about the products you like.

I like my laptop.

Oh yeah?

Yes, it's fast.

Word Partners

my favorite app

my favorite color

my favorite feature

my favorite place

my favorite product

my favorite thing

_____

GO ONLINE
to practice
word partners

Speaking Skill

Using *too* to express disappointment

Use *too* + an adjective to explain a problem with something. Listen to the examples.

Those glasses are **too expensive.** *They're not a good deal.*

This motorcycle is a little **too small.** *It can't carry more than one person, so I don't recommend it.*

My computer is **too old.** *I don't like it because I can't play games.*

C. Complete the sentences about things you own that you don't like. Then tell your partner about the products.

1. My _____ is too small.	
2. My _____ is too old.	I want a different one.
3. My _____ is too noisy.	I don't like it.
4. My _____ is too slow.	I need a new one.
5. My _____ is too heavy.	I think I'll get a new one.

Speaking Task

Reviewing a product and its features

1. Choose a product to review. Fill in the chart with information about a
product you like or do not like.

What is the product?	
What do you like about it?	
What do you not like about it?	
How many ☆s do you give it? (☆= not good, ☆☆☆☆☆ = excellent)	

2. Practice asking and answering the questions with a partner.

3. Work in a group. Close your books. Tell your group about your product. Give as
much information as you can. Listen to your partners' product reviews and ask
questions.

Step 3 REPORT

A. Review your partners' products. Write notes in the chart.

1. What product is more successful?	
2. What product is less successful?	

B. Share your notes. Which product has the best review for your group?

Step 4 REFLECT

Checklist

Check (✓) the things you learned in Chapter 8.

○ I learned language for talking about a product.

○ I understood a speaker saying how to use a product.

○ I gave a product review and wrote a report.

Discussion Question

How do customer reviews help businesses and customers?

- Use the simple past
- Listen for strong feelings with *really*
- Recognize *wasn't* and *weren't*
- Listen for past and present time signals
- Practice *-ed* endings
- Tell about a special possession

▲ VOCABULARY ▶ Oxford 2000 🔑 words to talk about special gifts

Learn Words

🔊 **A. Label each picture with the correct word. Then listen and repeat the words and phrases.**

| ~~college~~ | guitar | necklace | scooter | songs | souvenirs | stories | tool |

1.

saved money for ____college____

2.

told _____

3.

wore a pretty _____

4.

drove a _____

5.

sang _____

6.

bought cheap _____

7.

played _____

8.

used a special _____

Grammar Note

The simple past

🔊 Speakers use the simple past to talk about things that happened at a specific time in the past. Listen to the examples

*When I was a kid, I **played** the guitar.*

*My parents **bought** me a scooter last year.*

Regular verbs with *-ed*		Irregular verbs		
looked	saved	buy → bought	have → had	think → thought
loved	traveled	drive → drove	hear → heard	take → took
needed	wanted	give → gave	make → made	go → went
played	watched	get → got	sing → sang	wear → wore

🔊 **B. Listen and repeat.**

A

1. I saved time.
2. He used his hands.
3. We traveled together.
4. You knew this.
5. He bought a scooter.
6. It took three months.

B

I didn't save money.

He didn't use tools.

We didn't travel alone.

You didn't know that.

He didn't buy a car.

It didn't take long.

🔊 **C. Listen to each question. Circle the answer you hear.**

1. Did you play guitar as a kid? *Yes, I did.* (*No, I didn't.*)
2. Did your grandparents tell stories? *Yes, they did.* *No, they didn't.*
3. Did you walk to school? *Yes, I did.* *No, I didn't.*
4. What did your family do for fun? *We played games.* *We sang songs.*
5. Where did you live? *We lived in the city.* *We lived in a small town.*
6. When did you spend time with friends? *After school.* *On the weekends.*

💬 **D. Work with a partner. Ask and answer the questions in Activity C.**

Learn Phrases

A. Match each phrase to the correct picture. Then listen and repeat.

gave me a gift **when I finished college**	**had guests over** for dinner
played guitar **on the sidewalk**	**proud to own** a new car
reminds me of my family	shopped for **gold jewelry**
sold **used vehicles**	spent time with **both of my grandparents**

1.

2.

3.

4.

5.

6.

7.

8.

B. Listen to each conversation. Circle the correct answer.

1. They're talking about different   *kinds of vehicles.*   *kinds of tools.*

2. The woman is shopping for   *a used car.*   *a used guitar.*

3. The photo reminds him of   *his last vacation.*   *his grandparents.*

4. He's saving money   *for college.*   *for a scooter.*

5. His grandparents loved to   *share stories.*   *sing songs.*

C. Work with a partner. Think about your childhoods. Partner A asks a question. Partner B answers the question. Then partners switch roles.

1. Did your family tell stories?   *Yes, they told many stories.*   *No, not much.*

2. Did you sing songs?   *We sang a lot.*   *We didn't really sing.*

3. Did you have guests over?   *We had guests often.*   *Not a lot.*

4. Did you play soccer?   *Yes, I played all the time.*   *I didn't really like soccer.*

5. Did you ride a scooter?   *Yeah, I rode it everywhere.*   *Nope. I usually biked.*

6. Did you go shopping?   *I went a lot with my friends.*   *No, it wasn't my thing.*

> Did your family tell stories?

> Yes, they told many stories.

 D. Work with a partner. Use the words in the chart and your own ideas to ask and answer questions about your childhoods.

Partner A		Partner B
What did you do	with your friends?	We liked to...
	with your family?	We played...
	with your mom?	We rode...
	with your dad?	We often went...
	with your grandparents?	We told stories about...

> What did you do with your friends?

> We liked to go shopping together.

GO ONLINE for more practice

CONVERSATION

 A. Listen to the conversation. First listen for the main idea. Then listen again for the details. Write notes in the chart.

First listen: Main idea	Listen again: Details
What did Tim buy? _____	When did he buy it? _____ Why did he love it? _____ Why did he need it? _____

B. Work with a partner. Retell the story you heard. Use your ideas from Activity A.

GO ONLINE
for more
practice

Listening Strategy

Listening for strong feelings with *really*

Speakers use *really* to show that they feel strongly about something. Listen to the examples.

Use	Meaning
I **really** like it.	I like it a lot.
It was **really** fun.	It was a lot of fun.

C. Listen to the conversation again. Write the phrases you hear.

~~really cool~~	really hard	really glad	really love	really wanted

Alex: Hey, Tim, your new scooter's _____ *really cool* _____. I like the color.

Tim: Thanks! Red's my favorite color.

Alex: Where did you get it from?

Tim: I bought it from my neighbor. About a week ago.

Alex: So it's used?

Tim: It's used, but I _____ it. My neighbor didn't want it anymore. And

I _____ it. I loved the red. But I didn't have the money.

Alex: So what did you do?

Tim: I saved and saved. I worked _____. And finally, I bought it. I'm

_____ I did. Now I don't have to take the bus anymore.

Wasn't and *weren't*

Speakers use *was* and *were* with adjectives to describe people and things in the past. Use *was* for *I, it,* and singular nouns. Use *were* for *you, we, they,* and plural nouns. Listen to the examples.

> *My dad drove a scooter when I* **was** *a kid.*
>
> *Used scooters* **were** *hard to find.*

To make a negative statement, use *wasn't* and *weren't*. Listen to the examples.

> *My necklace* **wasn't** *cheap.*   *They* **weren't** *easy to find.*

To make questions, use *was/were* before the subject.

> **Was** *it expensive?*   *How old* **were** *you?*

D. Listen to each statement. Check (✓) the phrase you hear.

	A		B
1.	☐ was different	✓	were different
2.	☐ was special	☐	were special
3.	☐ wasn't new	☐	weren't new
4.	☐ where was	☐	when was
5.	☐ what were	☐	who were

E. Work with a partner. Use the words in the chart and your own ideas to ask and answer questions.

Partner A	Partner B
What was your life like when you were a kid? Tell me about your childhood.	My family was/wasn't big. I was/wasn't a good student. My parents were/weren't careful with money. There were/weren't a lot of kids in my neighborhood. We were/weren't always outside. Our house was/wasn't special.

Chant

GO ONLINE
for the
Chapter 9
Vocabulary &
Grammar Chant

A. Check (✓) the statements that are true for you. Then share your ideas with a partner.

☐ It's hard for me to choose gifts for my friends.

☐ Gifts from my family are very special to me.

☐ It makes me happy to give people gifts.

☐ Gifts remind me of important times in my life.

B. Listen to the first section. What is the speaker talking about? Circle the correct answer.

gifts from friends   *gifts from family*   *gifts from home*

C. Listen to the first and second sections. Circle the correct answers.

1. Where did his grandfather play his guitar?   *on the sidewalk*   *on the street*

2. What did the other people do?   *took pictures*   *sang songs*

3. How did his grandfather make everyone feel?   *happy*   *relaxed*

4. How does Tyler feel about his guitar?   *excited*   *proud*

Listening Strategy

Listening for past and present time signals

Speakers often use time markers to distinguish a shift from the past to the present. Speakers use *ago* to signal a past event.

                    ⌐past time signal
So, **a few years ago**, I started learning guitar.

Speakers use *now* and *today* to signal a change to the present. Listen to the example.

                    present time signal⌐
My grandfather gave his guitar to me. **Now** I can play it for other people.

GO ONLINE
for more
practice

D. Listen to the third section. Complete each statement with a time signal from the box.

| now | today | two years ago | when |

1. _____ I was a little girl, she let me wear it at family dinners.

2. So, _____, I finished college, and she gave me this box.

3. I think she remembered how much I loved it. So it means a lot to me

   _____.

4. That was a great story. Thanks, Lucy. _____, what's your story?

E. Listen to the whole show. Then ask and answer the questions with a partner.

Partner A	Partner B
1. When did Tyler get the guitar?	2. Who gave Tyler the guitar?
3. When did Lucy get the necklace?	4. Who gave Lucy the necklace?
5. How are Tyler and Lucy similar?	6. How are Tyler and Lucy different?

Discuss the Ideas

F. Think about gifts you got in the past. Use the words in the chart and your own ideas to explain when you got the gift and what it reminds you of.

Partner A	Partner B
A friend My father/mother My aunt gave me a… My uncle bought me a… My grandfather/mother	Oh? Was it for something special? Really? Tell me about it.

Partner A	Partner B
Yeah, she gave it to me because… Yes, we were close, and… Yes, it is special. Here's why…	Wow, that's really special. I understand why it's important to you.

Speaking Task Telling about a special possession

Step 1 PREPARE

Pronunciation Skill

-*ed* endings

🔊 Past tense verbs with -*ed* have different ending sounds. Verbs that end in /t/ or /d/ take an extra syllable. Listen to the examples.

1	1 - 2
I want a new bike. →	*I want**ed** a new bike.*

1 - 2	1 - 2 - 3
We decide today. →	*We decid**ed** last year.*

/t/
They work every day. → *My grandmother work**ed** every day.*

/d/
I play guitar. → *My grandfather play**ed** guitar.*

GO ONLINE
for more
practice

🔊 **A. Listen and repeat.**

A	B
1. want it	wanted it
2. need money	needed money
3. visit them	visited them
4. decide today	decided today
5. bike to school	biked to school
6. like jewelry	liked jewelry
7. ask her	asked her
8. work today	worked last year
9. play guitar	played guitar
10. save money	saved money
11. use tools	used tools
12. study English	studied English

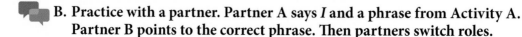 **B. Practice with a partner. Partner A says *I* and a phrase from Activity A. Partner B points to the correct phrase. Then partners switch roles.**

C. Listen. Complete each conversation with the correct forms of the verb. Then practice the conversations with a partner.

1. wait / waited

A: How long did you

    _____wait_____?

B: Maybe 20 minutes.

A: Really? We _____ for an hour.

3. start / started

A: Oh, no! The game

    _____ early today!

B: Don't worry. It didn't

    _____ without you.

A: Oh, good! I didn't want to miss the beginning.

5. bike / biked

A: I didn't _____ this weekend. It was too cold.

B: It's strange weather. Last weekend was beautiful.

A: I remember. I _____ both Saturday and Sunday.

2. visit / visited

A: Did your grandparents

    _____ you a lot?

B: Yes, they _____ every weekend.

A: How nice. What did you do together?

4. study / studied

A: I _____ English in high school.

B: Me, too. Did you

    _____ any other languages?

A: Yes, I learned a little French, too.

6. remind / reminded

A: What did the story

    _____ you of?

B: It _____ me of my childhood days.

A: Yeah, me, too, when life was much easier!

GO ONLINE
to practice the conversation

D. Work with a partner. Partner A says a statement. Partner B answers correctly. Then partners switch roles.

1. a. They ask a lot of questions.   That's because they're interested.
   b. They asked a lot of questions.   That's because they wanted to know more details.

2. a. I watch their games.   Do you watch them every week?
   b. I watched the game.   What a great game!

3. a. She talks a lot about it.   Well, she knows a lot about it.
   b. She talked a lot about it.   What did she say?

4. a. I want to go.   OK. Let's leave.
   b. I wanted to go.   Why didn't you leave?

5. a. They look tired.   I think they need some sleep.
   b. They looked tired.   Well, they played hard all day.

6. a. We like having guests over.   How often do you have guests?
   b. We liked having guests over.   I think everyone had a good time.

A. Think about things you own. Write an example for each idea in the chart.

a gift from someone	
something you bought for yourself	

 B. Tell a partner about your two objects from Activity A. Why is each object special to you?

Speaking Skill

Asking for extra details

🔊 When people listen to stories, they often want to know more details about the story. Speakers use *What kind(s) of* + noun to ask for extra details about objects and situations. Listen to the examples.

> A: *My aunt had beautiful jewelry.*
>
> B: **What kind of** <u>jewelry</u> *did she have?*
>
> A: *Mostly old jewelry.*

> A: *It was difficult for me to choose a car.*
>
> B: **What kinds of** <u>cars</u> *did you look at?*
>
> A: *Small trucks and some larger ones.*

Word Partners

really expensive

really fun

really happy

really important

really proud

really special

GO ONLINE
to practice
word partners

C. Complete the sentences about you.

1. When I was a child, my favorite gift was _____.

2. Last year, I shopped for _____.

3. One time, I gave my friend _____ as a gift.

4. I remember when I saved money to buy _____.

5. I bought _____ to remember my trip.

 D. Work with a partner. Partner A says a sentence from Activity C. Partner B asks *What kind(s) of* to get more details. Then partners switch roles.

> When I was a child, my favorite gift was a bicycle.

> What kind of bicycle was it?

> It was a mountain bike.

Speaking Task

Telling about a special possession

1. Fill in the chart with information about the special object you chose.

What is the object?	
How did you get it?	
Why is it special?	

2. Practice your presentation with a partner.

3. Close your book. Work in groups. Tell your story to your group. Then listen to the other stories and ask questions.

Step 3 REPORT

Write about one of the stories you heard. Answer the questions.

- Who is the speaker, and how did he or she get the object?

- Why is the object special to the speaker?

- How did the story make you feel?

Step 4 REFLECT

Checklist

Check (✓) the things you learned in Chapter 9.

○ I learned language for telling stories about special gifts and objects.

○ I understood a call-in show about special gifts from family.

○ I told a story about an object that is special to me.

Discussion Question

What was the best gift you gave someone? Why?

Look at the word bank for Unit 3. Check (✓) the words you know. Circle the words you want to learn better.

OXFORD 2000 ⚷

Adjectives	Nouns		Verbs
cheap	camera	market	buy
cool	car	motorcycle	choose
dark	change	pair	communicate
fast	college	past	deal
funny	customer	price	give
gold	experience	problem	find
light	feature	product	follow
low	fruit	rule	own
perfect	grandparent	shirt	recommend
proud	glasses	shoe	remember
used	guest	size	sell
	gift	song	share
	kitchen	story	sing
	jacket	tool	tell
	jewelry	vegetable	watch
	joke	vehicle	wear
	knife	video	

PRACTICE WITH THE OXFORD 2000 ⚷

A. Use the chart. Match adjectives with nouns.

1. _____a fast vehicle_____   2. _____

3. _____   4. _____

5. _____   6. _____

B. Use the chart. Match verbs with nouns.

1. _____choose a college_____   2. _____

3. _____   4. _____

5. _____   6. _____

C. Use the chart. Match verbs with adjective noun partners.

1. _____buy cheap glasses_____   2. _____

3. _____   4. _____

5. _____   6. _____

This is a list of the 2000 most important and useful words to learn at this stage in your language learning. These words have been carefully chosen by a group of language experts and experienced teachers, who have judged the words to be important and useful for three reasons.

- Words that are used very **frequently** (= very often) in English are included in this list. Frequency information has been gathered from the American English section of the Oxford English Corpus, which is a collection of written and spoken texts containing over 2 billion words.

- The keywords are frequent across a **range** of different types of text. This means that the keywords are often used in a variety of contexts, not just in newspapers or in scientific articles for example.

- The list includes some important words which are very **familiar** to most users of English, even though they are not used very frequently. These include, for example, words which are useful for explaining what you mean when you do not know the exact word for something.

Names of people, places, etc. beginning with a capital letter are not included in the list of 2000 keywords. Keywords which are not included in the list are numbers, days of the week, and the months of the year.

A

a, an *indefinite article*
ability *n.*
able *adj.*
about *adv., prep.*
above *prep., adv.*
absolutely *adv.*
academic *adj.*
accept *v.*
acceptable *adj.*
accident *n.*
   by accident
according to prep.
account *n.*
accurate *adj.*
accuse *v.*
achieve *v.*
achievement *n.*
acid *n.*
across *adv., prep.*
act *n., v.*
action *n.*
active *adj.*
activity *n.*
actor, actress *n.*
actual *adj.*
actually *adv.*
add *v.*
address *n.*
admire *v.*
admit *v.*
adult *n.*
advanced *adj.*
advantage *n.*
adventure *n.*
advertisement *n.*
advice *n.*

advise *v.*
affect *v.*
afford *v.*
afraid *adj.*
after *prep., conj., adv.*
afternoon *n.*
afterward *adv.*
again *adv.*
against *prep.*
age *n.*
   aged *adj.*
ago *adv.*
agree *v.*
agreement *n.*
ahead *adv.*
aim *n., v.*
air *n.*
airplane *n.*
airport *n.*
alarm *n.*
alcohol *n.*
alcoholic *adj.*
alive *adj.*
all *adj., pron., adv.*
allow *v.*
all right *adj., adv.,*
   exclamation
almost *adv.*
alone *adj., adv.*
along *prep., adv.*
alphabet *n.*
already *adv.*
also *adv.*
although *conj.*
always *adv.*
among *prep.*
amount *n.*

amuse *v.*
analyze *v.*
analysis *n.*
ancient *adj.*
and *conj.*
anger *n.*
angle *n.*
angry *adj.*
animal *n.*
announce *v.*
another *adj., pron.*
answer *n., v.*
any *adj., pron., adv.*
anymore *(also* any more*)*
   adv.
anyone *(also* anybody*)*
   pron.
anything *pron.*
anyway *adv.*
anywhere *adv.*
apart *adv.*
apartment *n.*
apparently *adv.*
appear *v.*
appearance *n.*
apple *n.*
apply *v.*
appointment *n.*
appreciate *v.*
appropriate *adj.*
approve *v.*
area *n.*
argue *v.*
argument *n.*
arm *n.*
army *n.*
around *adv., prep.*

arrange *v.*
arrangement *n.*
arrest *v.*
arrive *v.*
arrow *n.*
art *n.*
article *n.*
artificial *adj.*
artist *n.*
artistic *adj.*
as *prep., conj.*
ashamed *adj.*
ask *v.*
asleep *adj.*
at *prep.*
atmosphere *n.*
atom *n.*
attach *v.*
attack *n., v.*
attention *n.*
attitude *n.*
attract *v.*
attractive *adj.*
aunt *n.*
authority *n.*
available *adj.*
average *adj., n.*
avoid *v.*
awake *adj.*
aware *adj.*
away *adv.*

B

baby *n.*
back *n., adj., adv.*
backward *adv.*
bad *adj.*

badly *adv.*
bag *n.*
bake *v.*
balance *n.*
ball *n.*
band *n.*
bank *n.*
bar *n.*
base *n., v.*
baseball *n.*
basic *adj.*
basis *n.*
bath *n.*
bathroom *n.*
be *v.*
beach *n.*
bear *v.*
beard *n.*
beat *v.*
beautiful *adj.*
beauty *n.*
because *conj.*
become *v.*
bed *n.*
bedroom *n.*
beer *n.*
before *prep., conj., adv.*
begin *v.*
beginning *n.*
behave *v.*
behavior *n.*
behind *prep., adv.*
belief *n.*
believe *v.*
bell *n.*
belong *v.*
below *prep., adv.*
belt *n.*
bend *v.*
benefit *n.*
beside *prep.*
best *adj., adv., n.*
better *adj., adv.*
between *prep., adv.*
beyond *prep., adv.*
bicycle *n.*
big *adj.*
bill *n.*
bird *n.*
birth *n.*
birthday *n.*
bite *v.*
bitter *adj.*
black *adj.*
blame *v.*
block *n.*
blood *n.*
blow *v., n.*
blue *adj., n.*

board *n.*
boat *n.*
body *n.*
boil *v.*
bomb *n., v.*
bone *n.*
book *n.*
boot *n.*
border *n.*
bored *adj.*
boring *adj.*
born: be born *v.*
borrow *v.*
boss *n.*
both *adj., pron.*
bother *v.*
bottle *n.*
bottom *n.*
bowl *n.*
box *n.*
boy *n.*
boyfriend *n.*
brain *n.*
branch *n.*
brave *adj.*
bread *n.*
break *v.*
breakfast *n.*
breath *n.*
breathe *v.*
brick *n.*
bridge *n.*
brief *adj.*
bright *adj.*
bring *v.*
broken *adj.*
brother *n.*
brown *adj., n.*
brush *n., v.*
bubble *n.*
build *v.*
building *n.*
bullet *n.*
burn *v.*
burst *v.*
bury *v.*
bus *n.*
bush *n.*
business *n.*
busy *adj.*
but *conj.*
butter *n.*
button *n.*
buy *v.*
by *prep.*
bye *exclamation*

C

cabinet *n.*

cake *n.*
calculate *v.*
call *v., n.*
calm *adj.*
camera *n.*
camp *n., v.*
can *modal v., n.*
cancel *v.*
candy *n.*
capable *adj.*
capital *n.*
car *n.*
card *n.*
care *n., v.*
   take care of
   care for
career *n.*
careful *adj.*
carefully *adv.*
careless *adj.*
carelessly *adv.*
carry *v.*
case *n.*
   in case (of)
cash *n.*
cat *n.*
catch *v.*
cause *n., v.*
CD *n.*
ceiling *n.*
celebrate *v.*
cell *n.*
cell phone *n.*
cent *n.*
center *n.*
centimeter *n.*
central *adj.*
century *n.*
ceremony *n.*
certain *adj.*
certainly *adv.*
chain *n., v.*
chair *n.*
challenge *n.*
chance *n.*
change *v., n.*
character *n.*
characteristic *n.*
charge *n., v.*
charity *n.*
chase *v., n.*
cheap *adj.*
cheat *v.*
check *v., n.*
cheek *n.*
cheese *n.*
chemical *adj., n.*
chemistry *n.*
chest *n.*

chicken *n.*
chief *adj., n.*
child *n.*
childhood *n.*
chin *n.*
chocolate *n.*
choice *n.*
choose *v.*
church *n.*
cigarette *n.*
circle *n.*
citizen *n.*
city *n.*
class *n.*
clean *adj., v.*
clear *adj., v.*
clearly *adv.*
climate *n.*
climb *v.*
clock *n.*
close /kloʊs/ *adj., adv.*
close /kloʊz/ *v.*
closed *adj.*
cloth *n.*
clothes *n.*
clothing *n.*
cloud *n.*
club *n.*
coast *n.*
coat *n.*
coffee *n.*
coin *n.*
cold *adj., n.*
collect *v.*
collection *n.*
college *n.*
color *n., v.*
column *n.*
combination *n.*
combine *v.*
come *v.*
comfortable *adj.*
command *n.*
comment *n., v.*
common *adj.*
communicate *v.*
communication *n.*
community *n.*
company *n.*
compare *v.*
comparison *n.*
competition *n.*
complain *v.*
complaint *n.*
complete *adj.*
completely *adv.*
complicated *adj.*
computer *n.*
concentrate *v.*

concert *n.*
conclusion *n.*
condition *n.*
confidence *n.*
confident *adj.*
confuse *v.*
confused *adj.*
connect *v.*
connection *n.*
conscious *adj.*
consider *v.*
consist *v.*
constant *adj.*
contact *n., v.*
contain *v.*
container *n.*
continent *n.*
continue *v.*
continuous *adj.*
contract *n.*
contrast *n.*
contribute *v.*
control *n., v.*
convenient *adj.*
conversation *n.*
convince *v.*
cook *v.*
cookie *n.*
cooking *n.*
cool *adj.*
copy *n., v.*
corner *n.*
correct *adj., v.*
correctly *adv.*
cost *n., v.*
cotton *n.*
cough *v.*
could *modal v.*
count *v.*
country *n.*
county *n.*
couple *n.*
course *n.*
   of course
court *n.*
cousin *n.*
cover *v., n.*
covering *n.*
cow *n.*
crack *v.*
crash *n., v.*
crazy *adj.*
cream *n., adj.*
create *v.*
credit card *n.*
crime *n.*
criminal *adj., n.*
crisis *n.*
criticism *n.*

criticize *v.*
cross *v.*
crowd *n.*
cruel *adj.*
crush *v.*
cry *v.*
culture *n.*
cup *n.*
curly *adj.*
curve *n.*
curved *adj.*
custom *n.*
customer *n.*
cut *v., n.*

D

dad *n.*
damage *n., v.*
dance *n., v.*
dancer *n.*
danger *n.*
dangerous *adj.*
dark *adj., n.*
date *n.*
daughter *n.*
day *n.*
dead *adj.*
deal *v.*
dear *adj.*
death *n.*
debt *n.*
decide *v.*
decision *n.*
decorate *v.*
deep *adj.*
deeply *adv.*
defeat *v.*
definite *adj.*
definitely *adv.*
definition *n.*
degree *n.*
deliberately *adv.*
deliver *v.*
demand *n., v.*
dentist *n.*
deny *v.*
department *n.*
depend *v.*
depression *n.*
describe *v.*
description *n.*
desert *n.*
deserve *v.*
design *n., v.*
desk *n.*
despite *prep.*
destroy *v.*
detail *n.*
   in detail

determination *n.*
determined *adj.*
develop *v.*
development *n.*
device *n.*
diagram *n.*
dictionary *n.*
die *v.*
difference *n.*
different *adj.*
difficult *adj.*
difficulty *n.*
dig *v.*
dinner *n.*
direct *adj., adv., v.*
direction *n.*
directly *adv.*
dirt *n.*
dirty *adj.*
disadvantage *n.*
disagree *v.*
disagreement *n.*
disappear *v.*
disappoint *v.*
disaster *n.*
discover *v.*
discuss *v.*
discussion *n.*
disease *n.*
disgusting *adj.*
dish *n.*
dishonest *adj.*
disk *n.*
distance *n.*
distant *adj.*
disturb *v.*
divide *v.*
division *n.*
divorce *n., v.*
do *v., auxiliary v.*
doctor *n.* (*abbr.* Dr.)
document *n.*
dog *n.*
dollar *n.*
door *n.*
dot *n.*
double *adj.*
doubt *n.*
down *adv., prep.*
downstairs *adv., adj.*
downward *adv.*
draw *v.*
drawer *n.*
drawing *n*
dream *n., v.*
dress *n., v.*
drink *n., v.*
drive *v., n.*
driver *n.*

drop *v., n.*
drug *n.*
dry *adj., v.*
during *prep.*
dust *n.*
duty *n.*
DVD *n.*

E

each *adj., pron.*
each other *pron.*
ear *n.*
early *adj., adv.*
earn *v.*
earth *n.*
easily *adv.*
east *n., adj., adv.*
eastern *adj.*
easy *adj.*
eat *v.*
economic *adj.*
economy *n.*
edge *n.*
educate *v.*
education *n.*
effect *n.*
effort *n.*
e.g. *abbr.*
egg *n.*
either *adj., pron., adv.*
election *n.*
electric *adj.*
electrical *adj.*
electricity *n.*
electronic *adj.*
else *adv.*
e-mail (*also* email) *n., v.*
embarrass *v.*
embarrassed *adj.*
emergency *n.*
emotion *n.*
employ *v.*
employment *n.*
empty *adj.*
encourage *v.*
end *n., v.*
   in the end
enemy *n.*
energy *n.*
engine *n.*
enjoy *v.*
enjoyable *adj.*
enjoyment *n.*
enough *adj., pron., adv.*
enter *v.*
entertain *v.*
entertainment *n.*
enthusiasm *n.*
enthusiastic *adj.*

entrance *n.*
environment *n.*
equal *adj.*
equipment *n.*
error *n.*
escape *v.*
especially *adv.*
essential *adj.*
etc. *abbr.*
even *adv.*
evening *n.*
event *n.*
ever *adv.*
every *adj.*
everybody *pron.*
everyone *pron.*
everything *pron.*
everywhere *adv.*
evidence *n.*
evil *adj.*
exact *adj.*
exactly *adv.*
exaggerate *v.*
exam *n.*
examination *n.*
examine *v.*
example *n.*
excellent *adj.*
except *prep.*
exchange *v., n.*
excited *adj.*
excitement *n.*
exciting *adj.*
excuse *n., v.*
exercise *n.*
exist *v.*
exit *n.*
expect *v.*
expensive *adj.*
experience *n., v.*
experiment *n.*
expert *n.*
explain *v.*
explanation *n.*
explode *v.*
explore *v.*
explosion *n.*
expression *n.*
extra *adj., adv.*
extreme *adj.*
extremely *adv.*
eye *n.*

F

face *n., v.*
fact *n.*
factory *n.*
fail *v.*
failure *n.*

fair *adj.*
fall *v., n.*
false *adj.*
familiar *adj.*
family *n.*
famous *adj.*
far *adv., adj.*
farm *n.*
farmer *n.*
fashion *n.*
fashionable *adj.*
fast *adj., adv.*
fasten *v.*
fat *adj., n.*
father *n.*
fault *n.*
favor *n.*
    in favor
favorite *adj., n.*
fear *n., v.*
feather *n.*
feature *n.*
feed *v.*
feel *v.*
feeling *n.*
female *adj.*
fence *n.*
festival *n.*
few *adj., pron.*
    a few
field *n.*
fight *v., n.*
figure *n.*
file *n.*
fill *v.*
film *n.*
final *adj.*
finally *adv.*
financial *adj.*
find *v.*
    find out sth
fine *adj.*
finger *n.*
finish *v.*
fire *n., v.*
firm *n., adj.*
firmly *adv.*
first *adj., adv., n.*
    at first
fish *n.*
fit *v., adj.*
fix *v.*
fixed *adj.*
flag *n.*
flame *n.*
flash *v.*
flat *adj.*
flavor *n.*
flight *n.*

float *v.*
flood *n.*
floor *n.*
flour *n.*
flow *v.*
flower *n.*
fly *v.*
fold *v.*
follow *v.*
food *n.*
foot *n.*
football *n.*
for *prep.*
force *n., v.*
foreign *adj.*
forest *n.*
forever *adv.*
forget *v.*
forgive *v.*
fork *n.*
form *n., v.*
formal *adj.*
forward *adv.*
frame *n.*
free *adj., v., adv.*
freedom *n.*
freeze *v.*
fresh *adj.*
friend *n.*
friendly *adj.*
friendship *n.*
frighten *v.*
from *prep.*
front *n., adj.*
    in front
frozen *adj.*
fruit *n.*
fry *v.*
fuel *n.*
full *adj.*
fully *adv.*
fun *n., adj.*
funny *adj.*
fur *n.*
furniture *n.*
further *adj. , adv.*
future *n., adj.*

G

gain *v.*
gallon *n.*
game *n.*
garbage *n.*
garden *n.*
gas *n.*
gate *n.*
general *adj.*
    in general
generally *adv.*

generous *adj.*
gentle *adj.*
gently *adv.*
gentleman *n.*
get *v.*
gift *n.*
girl *n.*
girlfriend *n.*
give *v.*
glass *n.*
glasses *n.*
global *adj.*
glove *n.*
go *v.*
goal *n.*
god *n.*
gold *n., adj.*
good *adj., n.*
goodbye *exclamation*
goods *n.*
govern *v.*
government *n.*
grade *n., v.*
grain *n.*
gram *n.*
grammar *n.*
grandchild *n.*
grandfather *n.*
grandmother *n.*
grandparent *n.*
grass *n.*
grateful *adj.*
gray *adj., n.*
great *adj.*
green *adj., n.*
groceries *n.*
ground *n.*
group *n.*
grow *v.*
growth *n.*
guard *n., v.*
guess *v.*
guest *n.*
guide *n.*
guilty *adj.*
gun *n.*

H

habit *n.*
hair *n.*
half *n., adj., pron., adv.*
hall *n.*
hammer *n.*
hand *n.*
handle *v., n.*
hang *v.*
happen *v.*
happiness *n.*
happy *adj.*

hard *adj., adv.*
hardly *adv.*
harm *n., v.*
harmful *adj.*
hat *n.*
hate *v., n.*
have *v.*
   have to *modal v.*
he *pron.*
head *n.*
health *n.*
healthy *adj.*
hear *v.*
heart *n.*
heat *n., v.*
heavy *adj.*
height *n.*
hello *exclamation*
help *v., n.*
helpful *adj.*
her *pron., adj.*
here *adv.*
hers *pron.*
herself *pron.*
hide *v.*
high *adj., adv.*
highly *adv.*
high school *n.*
highway *n.*
hill *n.*
him *pron.*
himself *pron.*
hire *v.*
his *adj., pron.*
history *n.*
hit *v., n.*
hold *v., n.*
hole *n.*
holiday *n.*
home *n., adv..*
honest *adj.*
hook *n.*
hope *v., n.*
horn *n.*
horse *n.*
hospital *n.*
hot *adj.*
hotel *n.*
hour *n.*
house *n.*
how *adv.*
however *adv.*
huge *adj.*
human *adj., n.*
humor *n.*
hungry *adj.*
hunt *v.*
hurry *v., n.*
hurt *v.*

husband *n.*

I
I *pron.*
ice *n.*
idea *n.*
identify *v.*
if *conj.*
ignore *v.*
illegal *adj.*
illegally *adv.*
illness *n.*
image *n.*
imagination *n.*
imagine *v.*
immediate *adj.*
immediately *adv.*
impatient *adj.*
importance *n.*
important *adj.*
impossible *adj.*
impress *v.*
impression *n.*
improve *v.*
improvement *n.*
in *prep., adv.*
inch *n.*
include *v.*
including *prep.*
increase *v., n.*
indeed *adv.*
independent *adj.*
individual *adj.*
industry *n.*
infection *n.*
influence *n.*
inform *v.*
informal *adj.*
information *n.*
injure *v.*
injury *n.*
insect *n.*
inside *prep., adv., n., adj.*
instead *adv., prep.*
instruction *n.*
instrument *n.*
insult *v., n.*
intelligent *adj.*
intend *v.*
intention *n.*
interest *n., v.*
interested *adj.*
interesting *adj.*
international *adj.*
Internet *n.*
interrupt *v.*
interview *n.*
into *prep.*
introduce *v.*

introduction *n.*
invent *v.*
investigate *v.*
invitation *n.*
invite *v.*
involve *v.*
iron *n.*
island *n.*
issue *n.*
it *pron.*
item *n.*
its *adj.*
itself *pron.*

J
jacket *n.*
jeans *n.*
jewelry *n.*
job *n.*
join *v.*
joke *n., v.*
judge *n., v.*
judgment (*also*
   judgement) *n.*
juice *n.*
jump *v.*
just *adv.*

K
keep *v.*
key *n.*
kick *v., n.*
kid *n., v.*
kill *v.*
kilogram (*also* kilo) *n.*
kilometer *n.*
kind *n., adj.*
kindness *n.*
king *n.*
kiss *v., n.*
kitchen *n.*
knee *n.*
knife *n.*
knock *v., n.*
knot *n.*
know *v.*
knowledge *n.*

L
lack *n.*
lady *n.*
lake *n.*
lamp *n.*
land *n., v.*
language *n.*
large *adj.*
last *adj., adv., n., v.*
late *adj., adv.*
later *adv.*

laugh *v.*
laundry *n.*
law *n.*
lawyer *n.*
lay *v.*
layer *n.*
lazy *adj.*
lead /lid/ *v.*
leader *n.*
leaf *n.*
lean *v.*
learn *v.*
least *adj., pron., adv.*
   at least
leather *n.*
leave *v.*
left *adj., adv., n.*
leg *n.*
legal *adj.*
legally *adv.*
lemon *n.*
lend *v.*
length *n.*
less *adj., pron., adv.*
lesson *n.*
let *v.*
letter *n.*
level *n.*
library *n.*
lid *n.*
lie *v., n.*
life *n.*
lift *v.*
light *n., adj., v.*
lightly *adv.*
like *prep., v., conj.*
likely *adj.*
limit *n., v.*
line *n.*
lip *n.*
liquid *n., adj.*
list *n., v.*
listen *v.*
liter *n.*
literature *n.*
little *adj., pron., adv.*
a little
live /lɪv/ *v.*
living *adj.*
load *n., v.*
loan *n.*
local *adj.*
lock *v., n.*
lonely *adj.*
long *adj., adv.*
look *v., n.*
loose *adj.*
lose *v.*
loss *n.*

The Oxford 2000 List of Keywords

lost *adj.*
lot *pron., adv.*
  a lot (of)
  lots (of)
loud *adj.*
loudly *adv.*
love *n., v.*
low *adj., adv.*
luck *n.*
lucky *adj.*
lump *n.*
lunch *n.*

M

machine *n.*
magazine *n.*
magic *n., adj.*
mail *n., v.*
main *adj.*
mainly *adv.*
make *v.*
male *adj., n.*
man *n.*
manage *v.*
manager *n.*
many *adj., pron.*
map *n.*
mark *n., v.*
market *n.*
marriage *n.*
married *adj.*
marry *v.*
match *n., v.*
material *n.*
math *n.*
mathematics *n.*
matter *n., v.*
may *modal v.*
maybe *adv.*
me *pron.*
meal *n.*
mean *v.*
meaning *n.*
measure *v., n.*
measurement *n.*
meat *n.*
medical *adj.*
medicine *n.*
medium *adj.*
meet *v.*
meeting *n.*
melt *v.*
member *n.*
memory *n.*
mental *adj.*
mention *v.*
mess *n.*
message *n.*
messy *adj.*

metal *n.*
method *n.*
meter *n.*
middle *n., adj.*
midnight *n.*
might *modal v.*
mile *n.*
milk *n.*
mind *n., v.*
mine *pron.*
minute *n.*
mirror *n.*
Miss *n.*
miss *v.*
missing *adj.*
mistake *n.*
mix *v.*
mixture *n.*
model *n.*
modern *adj.*
mom *n.*
moment *n.*
money *n.*
month *n.*
mood *n.*
moon *n.*
moral *adj.*
morally *adv.*
more *adj., pron., adv.*
morning *n.*
most *adj., pron., adv.*
mostly *adv.*
mother *n.*
motorcycle *n.*
mountain *n.*
mouse *n.*
mouth *n.*
move *v., n.*
movement *n.*
movie *n.*
Mr. *abbr.*
Mrs. *abbr.*
Ms. *abbr.*
much *adj., pron., adv.*
mud *n.*
multiply *v.*
murder *n., v.*
muscle *n.*
museum *n.*
music *n.*
musical *adj.*
musician *n.*
must *modal v.*
my *adj.*
myself *pron.*
mysterious *adj.*

N

nail *n.*

name *n., v.*
narrow *adj.*
nation *n.*
national *adj.*
natural *adj.*
nature *n.*
navy *n.*
near *adj., adv., prep.*
nearby *adj., adv.*
nearly *adv.*
neat *adj.*
neatly *adv.*
necessary *adj.*
neck *n.*
need *v., n.*
needle *n.*
negative *adj.*
neighbor *n.*
neither *adj., pron., adv.*
nerve *n.*
nervous *adj.*
net *n.*
never *adv.*
new *adj.*
news *n.*
newspaper *n.*
next *adj., adv., n.*
nice *adj.*
night *n.*
no *exclamation, adj.*
nobody *pron.*
noise *n.*
noisy *adj.*
noisily *adv.*
none *pron.*
nonsense *n.*
no one *pron.*
nor *conj.*
normal *adj.*
normally *adv.*
north *n., adj., adv.*
northern *adj.*
nose *n.*
not *adv.*
note *n.*
nothing *pron.*
notice *v.*
novel *n.*
now *adv.*
nowhere *adv.*
nuclear *adj.*
number (*abbr.* No., no.) *n.*
nurse *n.*
nut *n.*

O

object *n.*
obtain *v.*
obvious *adj.*

occasion *n.*
occur *v.*
ocean *n.*
o'clock *adv.*
odd *adj.*
of *prep.*
off *adv., prep.*
offense *n.*
offer *v., n.*
office *n.*
officer *n.*
official *adj., n.*
officially *adv.*
often *adv.*
oh *exclamation*
oil *n.*
OK (*also* okay)
  exclamation, adj., adv.
old *adj.*
old-fashioned *adj.*
on *prep., adv.*
once *adv., conj.*
one *number, adj., pron.*
onion *n.*
only *adj., adv.*
onto *prep.*
open *adj., v..*
operate *v.*
operation *n.*
opinion *n.*
opportunity *n.*
opposite *adj., adv., n., prep.*
or *conj.*
orange *n., adj.*
order *n., v.*
ordinary *adj.*
organization *n.*
organize *v.*
organized *adj.*
original *adj., n.*
other *adj., pron.*
otherwise *adv.*
ought to *modal v.*
ounce *n.*
our *adj.*
ours *pron.*
ourselves *pron.*
out *adj., adv.*
out of *prep.*
outside *n., adj., prep., adv.*
oven *n.*
over *adv., prep.*
owe *v.*
own *adj., pron., v.*
owner *n.*

P

pack *v., n.*
package *n.*

page *n.*
pain *n.*
painful *adj.*
paint *n., v.*
painter *n.*
painting *n.*
pair *n.*
pale *adj.*
pan *n.*
pants *n.*
paper *n.*
parent *n.*
park *n., v.*
part *n.*
    take part (in)
particular *adj.*
particularly *adv.*
partly *adv.*
partner *n.*
party *n.*
pass *v.*
passage *n.*
passenger *n.*
passport *n.*
past *adj., n., prep., adv.*
path *n.*
patient *n., adj.*
pattern *n.*
pause *v.*
pay *v., n.*
payment *n.*
peace *n.*
peaceful *adj.*
pen *n.*
pencil *n.*
people *n.*
perfect *adj.*
perform *v.*
performance *n.*
perhaps *adv.*
period *n.*
permanent *adj.*
permission *n.*
person *n.*
personal *adj.*
personality *n.*
persuade *v.*
pet *n.*
phone *n.*
photo *n.*
photograph *n.*
phrase *n.*
physical *adj.*
physically *adv.*
piano *n.*
pick *v.*
    pick sth up
picture *n.*
piece *n.*

pig *n.*
pile *n.*
pilot *n.*
pin *n.*
pink *adj., n.*
pint *n.*
pipe *n.*
place *n., v.*
    take place
plain *adj.*
plan *n., v.*
plane *n.*
planet *n.*
plant *n., v.*
plastic *n.*
plate *n.*
play *v., n.*
player *n.*
pleasant *adj.*
please *exclamation, v.*
pleased *adj.*
pleasure *n.*
plenty *pron.*
pocket *n.*
poem *n.*
poetry *n.*
point *n., v.*
pointed *adj.*
poison *n., v.*
poisonous *adj.*
police *n.*
polite *adj.*
politely *adv.*
political *adj.*
politician *n.*
politics *n.*
pollution *n.*
pool *n.*
poor *adj.*
popular *adj.*
port *n.*
position *n.*
positive *adj.*
possibility *n.*
possible *adj.*
possibly *adv.*
post *n.*
pot *n.*
potato *n.*
pound *n.*
pour *v.*
powder *n.*
power *n.*
powerful *adj.*
practical *adj.*
practice *n., v.*
prayer *n.*
prefer *v.*
pregnant *adj.*

preparation *n.*
prepare *v.*
present *adj., n., v.*
president *n.*
press *n., v.*
pressure *n.*
pretend *v.*
pretty *adv., adj.*
prevent *v.*
previous *adj.*
price *n.*
priest *n.*
principal *n.*
print *v.*
priority *n.*
prison *n.*
prisoner *n.*
private *adj.*
prize *n.*
probable *adj.*
probably *adv.*
problem *n.*
process *n.*
produce *v.*
product *n.*
production *n.*
professional *adj.*
profit *n.*
program *n.*
progress *n.*
project *n.*
promise *v., n.*
pronunciation *n.*
proof *n.*
proper *adj.*
property *n.*
protect *v.*
protection *n.*
protest *n.*
proud *adj.*
prove *v.*
provide *v.*
public *adj., n.*
    publicly *adv.*
publish *v.*
pull *v.*
punish *v.*
punishment *n.*
pure *adj.*
purple *adj., n.*
purpose *n.*
    on purpose
push *v., n.*
put *v.*

Q
quality *n.*
quantity *n.*
quarter *n.*

queen *n.*
question *n., v.*
quick *adj.*
quickly *adv.*
quiet *adj.*
quietly *adv.*
quite *adv.*

R
race *n., v.*
radio *n.*
railroad *n.*
rain *n., v.*
raise *v.*
rare *adj.*
rarely *adv.*
rate *n.*
rather *adv.*
reach *v.*
reaction *n.*
read *v.*
ready *adj.*
real *adj.*
reality *n.*
realize *v.*
really *adv.*
reason *n.*
reasonable *adj.*
receive *v.*
recent *adj.*
recently *adv.*
recognize *v.*
recommend *v.*
record *n., v.*
recover *v.*
red *adj., n.*
reduce *v.*
refer to *v.*
refuse *v.*
region *n.*
regular *adj.*
regularly *adv.*
relation *n.*
relationship *n.*
relax *v.*
relaxed *adj.*
release *v.*
relevant *adj.*
relief *n.*
religion *n.*
religious *adj.*
rely *v.*
remain *v.*
remark *n.*
remember *v.*
remind *v.*
remove *v.*
rent *n., v.*
repair *v., n.*

repeat *v.*
replace *v.*
reply *n., v.*
report *v., n.*
reporter *n.*
represent *v.*
request *n., v.*
require *v.*
rescue *v.*
research *n., v.*
reservation *n.*
respect *n., v.*
responsibility *n.*
responsible *adj.*
rest *n., v.*
restaurant *n.*
result *n., v.*
return *v., n.*
rice *n.*
rich *adj.*
rid *v.*: get rid of
ride *v., n.*
right *adj., adv., n.*
ring *n., v.*
rise *n., v.*
risk *n., v.*
river *n.*
road *n.*
rob *v.*
rock *n.*
role *n.*
roll *n., v.*
romantic *adj.*
roof *n.*
room *n.*
root *n.*
rope *n.*
rough *adj.*
round *adj.*
route *n.*
row *n.*
royal *adj.*
rub *v.*
rubber *n.*
rude *adj.*
    rudely *adv.*
ruin *v.*
rule *n., v.*
run *v., n.*
rush *v.*

S
sad *adj.*
sadness *n.*
safe *adj.*
safely *adv.*
safety *n.*
sail *v.*
salad *n.*

sale *n.*
salt *n.*
same *adj., pron.*
sand *n.*
satisfaction *n.*
satisfied *adj.*
sauce *n.*
save *v.*
say *v.*
scale *n.*
scare *v.*
scared *adj.*
scary *adj.*
schedule *n.*
school *n.*
science *n.*
scientific *adj.*
scientist *n.*
scissors *n.*
score *n., v.*
scratch *v., n.*
screen *n.*
search *n., v.*
season *n.*
seat *n.*
second *adj., adv., n.*
secret *adj., n.*
secretary *n.*
secretly *adv.*
section *n.*
see *v.*
seed *n.*
seem *v.*
sell *v.*
send *v.*
senior *adj.*
sense *n.*
sensible *adj.*
sensitive *adj.*
sentence n.
separate *adj., v.*
separately *adv.*
series *n.*
serious *adj.*
serve *v.*
service *n.*
set *n., v.*
settle *v.*
several *adj., pron.*
sew *v.*
sex *n.*
sexual *adj.*
shade *n.*
shadow *n.*
shake *v.*
shame *n.*
shape *n., v.*
    shaped *adj.*
share *v., n.*

sharp *adj.*
she *pron.*
sheep *n.*
sheet *n.*
shelf *n.*
shell *n.*
shine *v.*
shiny *adj.*
ship *n.*
shirt *n.*
shock *n., v.*
shoe *n.*
shoot *v.*
shop *v.*
shopping *n.*
short *adj.*
shot *n.*
should *modal v.*
shoulder *n.*
shout *v., n.*
show *v., n.*
shower *n.*
shut *v.*
shy *adj.*
sick *adj.*
side *n.*
sight *n.*
sign *n., v.*
signal *n.*
silence *n.*
silly *adj.*
silver *n., adj.*
similar *adj.*
simple *adj.*
since *prep., conj., adv.*
sing *v.*
singer *n.*
single *adj.*
sink *v.*
sir *n.*
sister *n.*
sit *v.*
situation *n.*
size *n.*
skill *n.*
skin *n.*
skirt *n.*
sky *n.*
sleep *v., n.*
sleeve *n.*
slice *n.*
slide *v.*
slightly *adv.*
slip *v.*
slow *adj.*
slowly *adv.*
small *adj.*
smell *v., n.*
smile *v., n.*

smoke *n., v.*
smooth *adj.*
    smoothly *adv.*
snake *n.*
snow *n., v.*
so *adv., conj.*
soap *n.*
social *adj.*
society *n.*
sock *n.*
soft *adj.*
soil *n.*
soldier *n.*
solid *adj., n.*
solution *n.*
solve *v.*
some *adj., pron.*
somebody *pron.*
somehow *adv.*
someone *pron.*
something *pron.*
sometimes *adv.*
somewhere *adv.*
son *n.*
song *n.*
soon *adv.*
    as soon as
sore *adj.*
sorry *adj.*
sort *n., v.*
sound *n., v.*
soup *n.*
south *n., adj., adv.*
southern *adj.*
space *n.*
speak *v.*
speaker *n.*
special *adj.*
speech *n.*
speed *n.*
spell *v.*
spend *v.*
spice *n.*
spider *n.*
spirit *n.*
spoil *v.*
spoon *n.*
sport *n.*
spot *n.*
spread *v.*
spring *n.*
square *adj., n.*
stage *n.*
stair *n.*
stamp *n.*
stand *v., n.*
standard *n., adj.*
star *n.*
stare *v.*

start *v., n.*
state *n., v.*
statement *n.*
station *n.*
stay *v.*
steady *adj.*
steal *v.*
steam *n.*
step *n., v.*
stick *v., n.*
sticky *adj.*
still *adv., adj.*
stomach *n.*
stone *n.*
stop *v., n.*
store *n., v.*
storm *n.*
story *n.*
stove *n.*
straight *adv., adj.*
strange *adj.*
street *n.*
strength *n.*
stress *n.*
stretch *v.*
strict *adj.*
string *n.*
strong *adj.*
strongly *adv.*
structure *n.*
struggle *v., n.*
student *n.*
study *n., v.*
stuff *n.*
stupid *adj.*
style *n.*
subject *n.*
substance *n.*
succeed *v.*
success *n.*
successful *adj.*
successfully *adv.*
such *adj.*
　such as
suck *v.*
sudden *adj.*
suddenly *adv.*
suffer *v.*
sugar *n.*
suggest *v.*
suggestion *n.*
suit *n.*
suitable *adj.*
sum *n.*
summer *n.*
sun *n.*
supply *n.*
support *n., v.*
suppose *v.*

sure *adj., adv.*
surface *n.*
surprise *n., v.*
surprised *adj.*
surround *v.*
survive *v.*
swallow *v.*
swear *v.*
sweat *n., v.*
sweet *adj.*
swim *v.*
switch *n., v.*
symbol *n.*
system *n.*

T

table *n.*
tail *n.*
take *v.*
talk *v., n.*
tall *adj.*
tape *n.*
task *n.*
taste *n., v.*
tax *n.*
tea *n.*
teach *v.*
teacher *n.*
team *n.*
tear /tɛr/ *v.*
tear /tɪr/ *n.*
technical *adj.*
technology *n.*
telephone *n.*
television *n.*
tell *v.*
temperature *n.*
temporary *adj.*
tend *v.*
terrible *adj.*
test *n., v.*
text *n.*
than *prep., conj.*
thank *v.*
thanks *n.*
thank you *n.*
that *adj., pron., conj.*
the *definite article*
theater *n.*
their *adj.*
theirs *pron.*
them *pron.*
themselves *pron.*
then *adv.*
there *adv.*
therefore *adv.*
they *pron.*
thick *adj.*
thin *adj.*

thing *n.*
think *v.*
thirsty *adj.*
this *adj., pron.*
though *conj., adv.*
thought *n.*
thread *n.*
threat *n.*
threaten *v.*
throat *n.*
through *prep., adv.*
throw *v.*
thumb *n.*
ticket *n.*
tie *v., n.*
tight *adj., adv.*
time *n.*
tire *n.*
tired *adj.*
title *n.*
to *prep., infinitive marker*
today *adv., n.*
toe *n.*
together *adv.*
toilet *n.*
tomato *n.*
tomorrow *adv., n.*
tongue *n.*
tonight *adv., n.*
too *adv.*
tool *n.*
tooth *n.*
top *n., adj.*
topic *n.*
total *adj., n.*
totally *adv.*
touch *v., n.*
tour *n.*
tourist *n.*
toward *prep.*
towel *n.*
town *n.*
toy *n.*
track *n.*
tradition *n.*
traffic *n.*
train *n., v.*
training *n.*
translate *v.*
transparent *adj.*
transportation *n.*
trash *n.*
travel *v., n.*
treat *v.*
treatment *n.*
tree *n.*
trial *n.*
trick *n.*
trip *n., v.*

trouble *n.*
truck *n.*
true *adj.*
trust *n., v.*
truth *n.*
try *v.*
tube *n.*
tune *n.*
tunnel *n.*
turn *v., n.*
TV *n.*
twice *adv.*
twist *v.*
type *n., v.*
typical *adj.*

U

ugly *adj.*
unable *adj.*
uncle *n.*
uncomfortable *adj.*
unconscious *adj.*
under *prep., adv.*
underground *adj., adv.*
understand *v.*
underwater *adj., adv.*
underwear *n.*
unemployment *n.*
unexpected *adj.*
unexpectedly *adv.*
unfair *adj.*
unfortunately *adv.*
unfriendly *adj.*
unhappy *adj.*
uniform *n.*
union *n.*
unit *n.*
universe *n.*
university *n.*
unkind *adj.*
unknown *adj.*
unless *conj.*
unlikely *adj.*
unlucky *adj.*
unpleasant *adj.*
until *conj., prep.*
unusual *adj.*
up *adv., prep.*
upper *adj.*
upset *v., adj.*
upstairs *adv., adj.*
upward *adv.*
urgent *adj.*
us *pron.*
use *v., n.*
used *adj.*
used to *modal v.*
useful *adj.*
user *n.*

The Oxford 2000 List of Keywords

usual *adj.*
usually *adv.*

V

vacation *n.*
valley *n.*
valuable *adj.*
value *n.*
variety *n.*
various *adj.*
vary *v.*
vegetable *n.*
vehicle *n.*
very *adv.*
video *n.*
view *n.*
violence *n.*
violent *adj.*
virtually *adv.*
visit *v., n.*
visitor *n.*
voice *n.*
volume *n.*
vote *n., v.*

W

wait *v.*
wake (up) *v.*
walk *v., n.*
wall *n.*
want *v.*
war *n.*
warm *adj., v.*
warn *v.*
wash *v.*
waste *v., n., adj.*
watch *v., n.*
water *n.*
wave *n., v.*
way *n.*
we *pron.*
weak *adj.*
weakness *n.*
weapon *n.*
wear *v.*
weather *n.*
website *n.*
wedding *n.*
week *n.*
weekend *n.*
weigh *v.*
weight *n.*
welcome *v.*
well *adv., adj., exclamation*
    as well (as)
west *n., adj., adv.*
western *adj.*
wet *adj.*
what *pron., adj.*

whatever *adj., pron., adv.*
wheel *n.*
when *adv., conj.*
whenever *conj.*
where *adv., conj.*
wherever *conj.*
whether *conj.*
which *pron., adj.*
while *conj., n.*
white *adj., n.*
who *pron.*
whoever *pron.*
whole *adj., n.*
whose *adj., pron.*
why *adv.*
wide *adj.*
wife *n.*
wild *adj.*
will *modal v., n.*
win *v.*
wind /wɪnd/ *n.*
window *n.*
wine *n.*
wing *n.*
winner *n.*
winter *n.*
wire *n.*
wish *v., n.*
with *prep.*
within *prep.*
without *prep.*
woman *n.*
wonder *v.*
wonderful *adj.*
wood *n.*
wooden *adj.*
wool *n.*
word *n.*
work *v., n.*
worker *n.*
world *n.*
worried *adj.*
worry *v.*
worse *adj., adv.*
worst *adj., adv., n.*
worth *adj.*
would *modal v.*
wrap *v.*
wrist *n.*
write *v.*
writer *n.*
writing *n.*
wrong *adj., adv.*

Y

yard *n.*
year *n.*
yellow *adj., n.*
yes *exclamation*

yesterday *adv., n.*
yet *adv.*
you *pron.*
young *adj.*
your *adj.*
yours *pron.*
yourself *pron.*
youth *n.*